Training to be a Physician

A handbook of the
Royal College of Physicians of London

Third edition

Compiled by the New Consultants Committee
of the Royal College of Physicians

2001

ROYAL COLLEGE OF PHYSICIANS OF LONDON

Acknowledgements

We would like to thank the members of the Trainees Committee and the old Standing Committee of Members who contributed to early drafts of this latest edition. We would particularly like to thank all those individuals who provided original or revised articles and without whose contribution this book could not have been produced.

Royal College of Physicians of London
11 St Andrews Place, London NW1 4LE

Registered Charity No. 210508

Copyright © 2001 Royal College of Physicians of London
ISBN 1 86016 149 9

A catalogue record of this book is available from the British Library

Designed by Merriton Sharp, London
Printed in Great Britain by Sarum ColourView Group, Salisbury, Wiltshire

Contents

Introduction

These are challenging times! We are in the midst of unprecedented changes in medicine as the nation attempts to cope with ever-increasing demands on the NHS. The medical profession is not immune to these changes. Consultants no longer rule the roost and are part of teams with real responsibilities, not just to their patients but also to their employing Trust. Increasingly they work in teams and as partners with other health professionals. At the same time, stresses have never been greater with increasing accountability, demands for more openness, greater risks of litigation and an inexorable rise in workload. Within all of this we, of course, still need high-class, well-trained doctors. Training grades have also not been immune to change. We are currently re-examining the SHO grade, whilst we now have the Calman system for Specialist Registrar Training.

The current volume is designed for those wishing to have a career in medicine or one of its specialties. It contains valuable information on general topics such as the roles of the College and everything from the MRCP to applying for consultant appointments. In the second part are nutshell descriptions of training programmes in all the specialties. The volume is the fruit of much labour by the old Members Committee and now the New Consultants Committee. We hope that those of you looking for a consultant career in medicine will find it useful.

Professor Sir George Alberti
President, Royal College of Physicians of London

Part 1 Structures for training

CHAPTER 1

The role of the College in postgraduate medical education

The College has a central role nationally to promote and maintain the very highest standards of clinical practice. As part of that process, the College provides a forum for the exchange of ideas and up-to-date information on all aspects of medicine. The greater part of the content of the College educational programme relates to clinical practice, but there are also occasions each year when the results of current research are presented. Great emphasis is placed on the multi-disciplinary nature of College meetings and conferences, and there is frequent input from the College Faculties of Public Health Medicine, Occupational Medicine, Accident and Emergency Medicine and Pharmaceutical Medicine. There are also conferences and lectures covering aspects of medical ethics, clinical governance, health service management and the law. Further information about all these activities can be obtained from the Conference Office at the College.

Teach-ins

The teach-in programme has been designed primarily to provide a suitable framework for those studying for the MRCP examination. The College hosts monthly evening events covering broad clinical topics such as jaundice, respiratory failure and cardiac ischaemia, and similar teach-in programmes are now organised by several of the regional offices of the College. There is also a series of full day teaching events (the Regional Teach-ins) which are held throughout the year at the larger medical centres around the country.

Conferences

The majority of the conferences are held at the College, but in addition, each year the College hosts a major Regional Conference and contributes to (or co-hosts) overseas conferences and joint conferences with other UK-based Royal Colleges.

General Conferences

A highlight in the College calendar is the Advanced Medicine conference, which is held over four days, and covers a wide range of clinical topics. There are many 'state-of-the-art' clinical reviews, but the scope of the meeting also includes an examination of the impact of recent developments in laboratory, clinical and health services research. The proceedings are published as a book in the series *Horizons in Medicine*.

Several conferences are organised jointly with other colleges and faculties, and these include an annual Paediatric conference, joint conferences with the Scottish Royal Colleges, and meetings with one or more of the Medical Faculties. The themes covered in these events are mainly clinical, but input is sought also from public figures and specialists in occupational and public health, the social sciences, politics and the law.

At the other end of the clinical spectrum, the College hosts the annual Science and Medicine conference, at which the objective is to anticipate the likely changes in clinical practice that might follow current laboratory-based and clinical research. The meetings are held over two days and comprise short presentations by those engaged in research, as well as more general reviews giving an update within a particular area.

Conferences on specific subjects

College conferences often focus on a particular theme. The purpose of these events is to draw together expertise from the many related clinical and non-clinical disciplines to address important topics. Examples might include stroke rehabilitation, alcohol and the young, travel medicine or ethical issues at the end of life.

The College welcomes suggestions for future conferences from its Members, Fellows and relevant organisations involved in healthcare. Many years experience has shown that our most successful events are not those that duplicate the efforts of the specialist medical societies, but rather those conferences that bring together doctors and related clinical staff from all fields of medical practice, NHS administrators, social scientists and members of government.

Lectures

Generous bequests to the College over the last 480 years have provided opportunities to extend the extensive programme of named College Lectures. Many are delivered as part of College conferences both in London and elsewhere. A few, such as the Harveian Oration, are hosted by the College as free-standing events, and may be of interest to physicians-in-training.

Royal College of Physicians publications

The College publishes a wide variety of publications. Those directed specifically to the postgraduate readership include:

▶ *Clinical Medicine: The Journal of the Royal College of Physicians of London*. Published bi-monthly, *Clinical Medicine* complements the role of the College in seeking to maintain high standards of patient care and medical education. It includes original papers, review articles and College lectures on the practice of internal medicine and carries editorials on current issues surrounding medicine and medical education and ethics. The journal also contains a Continuing Medical Education (CME) section which will cover all the specialties systematically, one specialty being covered over two issues. CME points are awarded for responses to a self-assessment questionnaire based on this section that is included with each journal.

▶ edited proceedings of selected conferences are published as soft cover books. Of these, the series of books *Horizons in Medicine*, based on the annual Advanced Medicine Conference, is particularly relevant to physicians who wish to update themselves in cutting-edge medicine over a wide range of specialties.

▶ other educational material, working party reports on medical topics of current interest and debate and clinical guidelines are also published by the College.

▶ advanced notice of all academic activities is published in the College Commentary which is circulated to Fellows and Members three times each year.

CHAPTER 2

The MRCP(UK) examination

The MRCP(UK) Examination is owned and managed by the Federation of Royal Colleges of the United Kingdom. The Examination binds together three institutions with common aims:

The Royal College of Physicians of Edinburgh
The Royal College of Physicians & Surgeons of Glasgow
The Royal College of Physicians of London

It was established when a joint Examination Board of the three Royal Colleges was set up and a Common Part 1 Examination was introduced in 1968. A Common Part 2 Examination was introduced in 1972 and the award of MRCP(UK) established. This was an important action by the three Royal Colleges of Physicians and has been consolidated in many other areas subsequently with the most recent being a common approach to CPD.

In the UK the MRCP(UK) is a prerequisite for physicians wishing to undergo higher training in a medically related specialty. The aim of the MRCP(UK) Examination is to identify those physicians who, having undertaken a period of general training, have acquired the necessary professional knowledge, skills and attitudes to enable them to benefit from a programme of higher specialist training.

The Examination therefore plays an essential role in the overall educational experience and continuing professional development of physicians in the UK. It is often the first point of contact that trainees have with the Royal Colleges of Physicians.

The MRCP(UK) Examination also plays an increasingly important role in the international arena of medical education. It serves to provide a professional standard against which physicians working overseas may measure their level of attainment. It is also being used by medical educationalists in other countries in respect of local postgraduate assessments.

During the life of the MRCP(UK) Diploma there has been a process of continual audit and modification. In spite of the acknowledged high standing of the MRCP(UK) there has been criticism both from within the

Colleges and from a number of authorities in medical education. Prompted by these views, in 1996 the MRCP(UK) Policy Committee sought and obtained authority from the Federation of Royal Colleges of Physicians of the UK to undertake a major review of the Examination. The underlying principle guiding the Review process was a commitment to base any recommended changes on sound educational principles to improve further the objectivity and fairness of the Examination. It was also agreed that a robust administrative system was required to cope with the demands of these changes and developments. The following recommendations from the Review were implemented by 1999:

i   The aims and objectives of the Examination have been agreed and published;
ii   A syllabus for the Part 1 Examination has been published;
iii Clinical Guidelines for the Part 1 Examination have been published;
iv   Past MRCP(UK) Examination Papers have been revised and published;
v   Training and briefing for examiners has been introduced;
vi   Information about the Examination has been made more widely available;
vii Candidates now have an unlimited number of attempts at the Part 1 and Part 2 Examinations, provided that all other Regulations are met;
viii Candidates scoring a mark of 9 in the Part 2 Written Paper now pass the Part 2 Examination if they achieve an overall Part 2 mark of 25;
ix   Candidates who have been unsuccessful in the Examination are given more feedback about their performance;
x   Introduction of a Validation, Audit and Research Group (VARG) to compliment the work of the Examining Boards.

The conversion of the IT system to a stable platform was also completed on time and within budget.

This has enabled two significant developments to take place recently:

i   The establishment of a free-standing Part 2 Written Examination;
ii   The introduction of a separate Clinical Examination known as the Practical Assessment of Clinical Examination Skills (PACES). Candidates passing the Part 2 Written Examination will be permitted a period of two years in which to pass PACES, before being required to re-sit the written section. The Oral Examination has now disappeared. The timetable for the MRCP(UK) has needed to be modified to cope with these developments but candidates are now given a much greater degree of flexibility when taking the MRCP(UK).

The PACES exam consists of five 'stations' which the candidates will move around. Performance at each of the stations is assessed by two independent examiners who have structured marking sheets. Three of the stations test clinical knowledge; one tests history-taking skills; and one communications skills and ethics. The new exam is more objective than the previous Part 2, and will relate much more closely to real clinical situations.

Work will commence on introducing Criterion Referencing (standard setting) as the means for assessing the Part 1 and Part 2 Written Examination, replacing the peer referenced marking system. The introduction of criterion referenced marking will coincide with the discontinuation of the system of negative marking in the Part 1 Examination. The format of the Part 1 and Part 2 Written Examination will develop over the course of 2002 and candidates are advised to watch for notices in the MRCP(UK) Regulations and Application Forms that will detail these changes.

It is intended to develop the profile of MRCP(UK) publications even further by regular publication of past examination papers, provision of syllabuses and the development of an MRCP(UK) Examination web site.

In an examination of high quality, reliability is essential and statistical information is available to the Examining Boards at the completion of each examination. The Validation Audit and Research Group has continued with its role of auditing the Examination and, having defined its aims and objectives, is now starting to carry out research.

The Federation of the Royal Colleges of Physicians believe that the MRCP(UK) is but the beginning of a lifelong educational process for those following a career in medicine and its sub-specialties. As such, they see it as vitally important that the Examination remains relevant to modern medical practice. The Examination will continue to evolve long after the current changes and as medical and educational practice dictate.

CHAPTER 3

The role of the College tutor

Where does the College tutor fit into the postgraduate medical education hierarchy? College tutors are appointed by, and are responsible to, the Royal College of Physicians (RCP); their role includes:

▶ representing the interest of the RCP and providing a link between the hospital/Trust and the RCP Regional and Deputy Regional Advisers and Regional Postgraduate Deans

▶ promoting education and training within their Trust

▶ ensuring a regular programme of appraisal and assessment takes place for SHOs

▶ providing career advice

▶ arranging and co-ordinating locally General Professional Training External Assessor and Interim Reviews with the GPT Office and Regional Adviser

The Clinical tutor, on the other hand, is responsible to the postgraduate dean and is appointed by the dean after local consultation. At Trust level, the Clinical tutor has overall responsibility for *facilitation* of postgraduate educational activities across different specialties (see Figure 1).

The College appoints tutors throughout England, Wales and Northern Ireland. Their first task should be to advertise their existence. Every acute Trust should have a programme of postgraduate educational activities and the College tutor should ensure that his or her name appears on the front page of this programme alongside the names of the other 'specialty tutors' responsible to the other Royal colleges, eg surgery, psychiatry, radiology etc. The names of these 'specialty tutors' should also appear on a list in the postgraduate centre in each hospital, and should be readily available from the postgraduate secretary. If the name of the College tutor is not readily available, junior doctors should be encouraged to enquire from the local postgraduate secretary to ascertain the identity of the College tutor, and when he or she might be available to give advice.

Figure 1 Postgraduate medical educational hierarchies

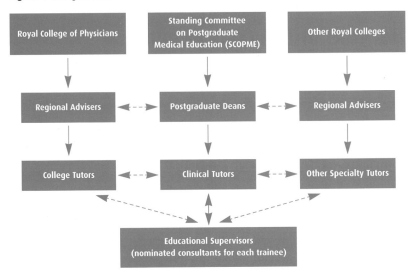

RCP Associate College tutors

The role of the Associate tutor

The role of the Associate tutor provides an opportunity for involvement with the educational activities of the College as well as with local teaching and training matters. Their role includes:

▶ representing their fellow trainees
▶ working with the RCP tutor in all aspects of training and education of SHOs
▶ assisting with the dissemination of information from the RCP and assisting with publishing of College events
▶ assisting in the organisation of College visits to assess SHO training

Like the College tutor, their first task should be to ensure that their name is made known to the SHOs via the postgraduate centre notice board and education programmes organised for SHO training.

The Associate tutor must be a physician in training and be nominated by the RCP tutor in consultation with the trainee physicians at the hospital concerned.

From whom should a junior doctor receive advice?

Faced with a seeming embarrassment of riches in terms of people available to give postgraduate advice, it is surprising that most junior doctors, when surveyed, say that there is no one to give them such advice. They should be encouraged to discuss problems with their own consultant who, in some circumstances, may also be their educational supervisor. More often than not, satisfactory advice can be obtained at this first port of call. However, in circumstances where further advice is required, there is a hierarchy that can be followed (Table 1). Where the problems relate to postgraduate medical education, for example in relation to the MRCP(UK) examination, the next person to consult should be the College tutor. If, however, the College tutor also happens to be the first person on the list, ie the junior doctor's own consultant, the Clinical tutor may also be consulted. If even that gives no satisfaction, the RCP Regional Adviser and/or the Regional Postgraduate Dean can be consulted.

It goes without saying that there is a wealth of knowledge available within the pool of junior doctors and it will pay each individual to develop a network to access this advice. However, more senior advice should usually be sought to confirm and amplify the 'conventional wisdom'.

Table 1 Hierarchy for a junior doctor to seek advice

1 Consultant (educational supervisor)	4 Clinical tutor
2 Associate College tutor	5 Regional adviser
3 College tutor	6 Regional Postgraduate Dean

Career guidance

Consultants think that career guidance happens routinely, yet SHOs will say that it does not. Again, it is the College tutor's and the Clinical tutor's responsibility to make career guidance available within the Trust. Most junior doctors should be advised to follow the hierarchy as set out in Table 2; however, one additional important source of information is, as mentioned above, their peer group. It is very important that they should also discuss careers not only with their SHO colleagues but also with Specialist Registrars in the appropriate speciality.

MRCP examination advice

Although this advice may be also sought from various sources within the local hospital, again perhaps following the hierarchy in Table 2, the

College tutor is certainly the major source of information within the individual hospital. An SHO who is contemplating sitting the MRCP(UK) examination may seek advice from the College tutor, who can recommend the appropriate information published by the College about the examination, and would also be able to answer questions regarding what it entails, when to sit the examination, and what is appropriate in the way of study leave or courses. The College tutor will have negotiated a local policy on study leave with the Clinical tutor, who is responsible for signing study leave forms and, through the Regional Postgraduate Dean, has access to the relevant budget. Within the hospital, the College tutor is likely to be responsible for organising MRCP teaching, which may be either a locally run course or ward-based, individual teaching, or a combination of these.

Needs of junior doctors

Appraisal & assessment

There are many differences between the two processes, but essentially *assessment* determines career progression whereas *appraisal* supports personal and professional development. It is important to note the difference between assessment and appraisal.

An appraisal is the process of collecting information about the individual SHO, followed by a dialogue between the SHO and the appraiser for the purpose of reviewing performance over a range of areas and over a period of time. It is entirely for the benefit of the SHO and is intended to identify educational needs, to assess progress and career development and give advice and support. It should be a one-to-one encounter with the educational supervisor at the beginning, middle and end of each training post. Appraisal provides an opportunity to discuss future goals and to review individual learning plans with the educational supervisor. The RCP SHO Appraisal Record will be of considerable help in this process.

Assessment is the process of measuring or describing competence and performance against defined criteria based on relevant content. It is an opportunity to check progress on a regular basis (usually annually) against the Core Curriculum. This is intended to provide support and to guide trainees and trainers of the requirements of the post and assess whether the required standards are being achieved. It provides feedback from the trainee to the educational supervisor on the quality of posts and training programmes. Assessments involve scrutiny of training records.

Local Postgraduate Medical Education Committees

Most Trusts have a Postgraduate Education Committee which is chaired by the Clinical tutor and usually has as members:

▶ Specialty tutors who are responsible to all the Royal colleges
▶ representatives of the undergraduate dean from the local university
▶ two junior doctors
▶ a management representative from the personnel department

Trusts should be encouraged to have a sub-committee looking specifically at the educational programme for SHOs. They should ensure delivery of the educational programme in 'bleep-free' time and regularly review its content, which should be based on the SHO core curriculum and be given an MRCP examination focus. In some Trusts, the larger educational committee may have lapsed, but an SHO Educational Programme Committee should still be formed under the aegis of the College Tutor.

Educational contracts

After initial appraisal meetings with their educational supervisors, SHOs should be encouraged to devise personal learning plans. The targets of learning plans should form the basis of the 'educational agreement'. This agreement will include the study leave that is required, together with the support the SHO will need, to achieve these targets. The agreement should then be signed by both the educational supervisor and the SHO. Again, the SHO Appraisal Record should help in this process.

General educational role of the College tutor

The precise extent of the role of the College tutor depends on whether or not the Clinical tutor is also a physician, and it will probably be the College tutor's responsibility to facilitate regular educational meetings, such as specific topic seminars, journal clubs, weekly physicians' meetings (grand rounds) and other protected-time teaching for doctors in training. This may include delivery of the core curriculum for SHOs. It is likely that the College tutor and the Clinical tutor will discuss the integration of clinico-pathological meetings and audit, using both as educational tools. The College tutor will be one of the Clinical tutor's chief allies in exploring ways of changing our traditional teacher-centred methods of education and concentrating more on the needs of the learner.

Conclusion

The role of the College tutor may have many ramifications, but the education, appraisal and guidance of the physician in training should be the pivot of his or her activities. From the College tutor's point of view, this is likely to be satisfying but time consuming. Although education itself should be seen as part of the curriculum for a junior hospital doctor, and should be scheduled to happen between 9am and 5pm, it is likely that the role of the College tutor will extend to evenings and weekends, or, to misquote Thomas à Kempis: *sic transit gloria Sunday*.

CHAPTER 4

The role of the regional adviser

The College has an adviser in each region (deanery) in England, Wales and Northern Ireland. They are practising physicians, elected by local Fellows. They serve for six years, the first two as deputy regional adviser, before becoming adviser for two years. The last two years are spent as advisers for Continuing Professional Development.

Regional specialty advisers

The changes in higher specialist training made it necessary for postgraduate deans to identify experts in each medical specialty who could be consulted about education and training. These individuals also provide advice to the College on subjects such as standards of practice and job descriptions. Regional specialty advisers are appointed in consultation with the postgraduate dean or specialist society as appropriate.

Main activities of regional advisers

Liaison with Fellows and Members in the region

The regional adviser, who can be consulted by any Member or Fellow in the region, maintains close contact with the College tutors in order to keep Fellows, Members and others in the region informed of College policy and actions and, in turn, brings to the College regional opinion, ideas, doubts, suggestions and criticism. Meetings with College tutors and associate College tutors (who are trainees) generally take place locally two or three times each year.

Meetings of regional advisers

The regional advisers and their deputies meet quarterly at the College. The President chairs the meeting, which is also attended by the College officers, and representatives of the Censors (responsible for the MRCP(UK) examination) and of Council. Any regional adviser can add any subject to the agenda. Although the function of the meeting is advisory only, its influence is considerable.

Membership of regional specialist training committees
Each specialty has a regional training committee which informs and advises the postgraduate dean on all matters relating to higher medical training. The regional advisers are *ex officio* members of these committees, which usually meet twice a year. Although full members, their main responsibilities are to listen to the problems that concern the College and to try to interpret College recommendations and views. The regional advisers have direct access to the postgraduate deans and the considerable resources of the College. With the constant changes in the NHS, regional advisers' opinions are frequently sought.

Advisers, acting as regional specialty advisers in general (internal) medicine, chair the local training committee, nominate assessors in general (internal) medicine on the annual RITA reviews and oversee higher specialist training in general (internal) medicine.

Consultant appointments
The College nominates Fellows to serve as the College representative on consultant appointments committees (advisory appointments committees) in medical specialties. Before a consultant post is advertised, it must be approved by the regional Adviser, who is responsible for assessing all aspects of the proposed post, particularly the facilities available and junior staff support. He or she will almost invariably seek independent specialist advice, usually from the appropriate regional specialty adviser.

Specialist registrar appointments
The regional advisers are also involved in the appointment of specialist registrars in medical specialties. There is no formal representation of the College on these statutory committees, but most regions ask the regional adviser to nominate a representative.

Nominations for Fellowship
Members of the College may be nominated for the Fellowship once a year, the closing date being 1st September. Soon after this date, the regional advisers receive the list of nominations for their regions. They make enquiries among the Fellows to determine the support for these nominations and then transmit their findings to the College.

General Professional and Higher Specialist Training
Senior house officer posts must be approved for General Professional Training (GPT) before being advertised. The GPT office in the College

maintains a list of recognised posts which is circulated to advisers to ensure that reassessment by a visit takes place when recognition is due for review, usually after four years. These visits are conducted by assessors from outside the region, timed increasingly to coincide with the annual visit by the postgraduate dean. The regional advisers monitor the recommendations of the visiting team, in liaison with the postgraduate dean, the visit being organised by the local College tutor in collaboration with the clinical tutor and local clinicians. The regional advisers will be asked to ensure the recommendations made following a College visit are implemented. This may entail undertaking an interim visit to the Trust and submitting a further report to the GPT office. The regional advisers are not responsible for approval of posts for higher medical training, which is organised directly by the Joint Committee for Higher Medical Training (JCHMT), although they may be members of a visiting team.

College Continuing Medical Education advisers

With the introduction by the College of the formal Continuing Medical Education (CME) scheme in 1995, subsequently called Continuing Professional Development (CPD), regional advisers assumed responsibility for CPD activities in their territories. Liaising closely with the College CPD office, regional advisers act as a contact point for all aspects of CPD, as well as scrutinising and approving local requests for internal and external CPD accreditation. Regional advisers, after completing their term of office, become CPD advisers. Meetings of CPD advisers are held at the College three times a year, chaired by the Director of CPD.

Other activities

The regional advisers work closely with postgraduate deans on all aspects of training. They may be asked to advise managerial or clinical colleagues on professional matters, such as standards of care or provision of resources, or be consulted about job descriptions for non-consultant career grade staff. Junior medical staff who are having difficulty in passing the MRCP (UK) examination or who are experiencing other problems with their training may require counselling and advice on career prospects. College tutors are appointed by the College upon the nomination of regional advisers after consultation with local physicians, the clinical tutor and the postgraduate dean.

Periodically, regional advisers are involved with the collection of information for the College, for example, manpower data and current aspects of clinical medicine. In conjunction with the College tutors they are responsible for encouraging appropriate audit activities in each district. They also co-ordinate and promote regional College conferences, teach-ins and lectures, and are likely to have an important role in the co-ordination of clinical governance.

The establishment of the regional adviser network has been very successful, so much so that it is the College's intention to open a regional office in each deanery to provide direct support for regional advisers, thereby strengthening links with local Fellows and Members and the postgraduate deans.

CHAPTER 5

Postgraduate training

Readers will find full details of postgraduate training on the JCHMT section of the College website (www.rcplondon.ac.uk/jchmt).

General Professional Training

General Professional Training (GPT) is intended to provide experience in a wide range of specialties in order to assist with professional development and the choice of a future career. It is not exclusively for those intent on a career as a hospital physician; the broad based experience and training are of considerable value to those planning careers in a wide range of clinical, laboratory and administration-based specialties. Senior house officer (SHO) posts are also educationally approved for General Practice Vocational Training Schemes (GPVTS).

GPT is undertaken immediately after full registration and lasts for a minimum period of two years. In England, Wales and Northern Ireland, responsibility for approving posts for GPT is held by the Specialist Training Authority (STA) of the Medical Royal Colleges, which is devolved down to the Medical Royal Colleges.

Definition and specialty content of GPT

GPT occupies a minimum period of two years. It is usually obtained in a series of SHO posts approved by one of the Royal Colleges. The entry requirements for higher medical training include satisfactory completion of GPT and also a postgraduate diploma. This is usually MRCP (UK or I), but in some specialties other diplomas may fulfil the entry requirement, eg MRCOG in genito-urinary medicine.

The object of this period is to enable the trainee to obtain a broad medical experience and to identify the specialty which he/she hopes ultimately to follow. Some trainees make an early career choice, while others defer their decision until they have more experience. For this reason many doctors elect to spend longer than two years in the SHO grade, either to increase their clinical experience or to obtain additional training in a particular specialty before applying for specialist registrar posts.

Because of intense competition in the popular specialties, trainees must retain the option of making a change of career direction. Therefore, in addition to undertaking posts providing experience in general internal medicine (GIM) and its specialties, trainees may choose to gain experience in other disciplines. Such experience can be obtained in SHO graded posts, not necessarily restricted to the hospital medical specialties. Periods of up to six months in general practice or in departments of pathology, psychiatry, surgery or obstetrics and gynaecology are recognised as acceptable experience. At least 18 months should be spent in posts involved in the care of emergency admissions, which must include cardiac patients, and of which six months should involve unselected emergency takes.

Trainees in GIM should spend not more than six months in each post confined to a single specialty or attached to one team of consultants. Each SHO post attracts a maximum of six months' educational credit that can count towards the minimum requirement of two years in order to complete GPT. A longer period of time spent in a single specialty post will not count towards this requirement because training at this level requires the SHO to experience a broad range of general medical specialties. The *Guide for trainees and trainers*, outlining the requirements for completion of GPT can be obtained from the GPT office at the College.

The College is currently supporting the Chief Medical Officer's initiative to promote a five-year GIM programme, starting with a year of generic training and leading to a Certificate of Completion of Specialist Training (CCST) after a further four years in the training programme.

Approval of posts

All junior hospital posts require educational approval if they are to be filled by doctors in training. Since the standards required by the Royal College of Physicians for GPT and those for vocational training for general practice by the Royal College of Practitioners are so similar, a system of joint approval by both Colleges has been established. Hospital visits are carried out by teams with representatives from each College.

The visiting team normally consists of two assessors nominated by the Royal College of Physicians (one of whom will act as a chairperson), as well as a nominated representative of the Royal College of General Practitioners. The regional adviser and the deputy regional adviser of the Royal College of Physicians are usually present but are to be regarded as observers; the report is solely that of the assessors.

It is now common practice for the RCP to visit jointly with the regional postgraduate dean so that the dean's opinion can be sought about the report on the day of the visit and a reduction made in the number of visits a hospital need host.

Visiting teams are asked to look critically at the provision of educational facilities and the time available for study. Before recommending approval of posts, they should be satisfied that the programme is appropriate and that trainees are encouraged and permitted by their consultants to attend regularly. The Director of training at the RCP submits the reports of visiting teams to the sub committee of Council on GPT which confirms or modifies the recommendations of the visitors. Final approval of SHO posts for GPT is granted by Council.

Higher medical training

The introduction of the specialist registrar (SpR) grade has radically changed training for specialists in medicine. The main details of training arrangements can be found in *A guide to specialist registrar training* published by the Department of Health in February 1998. All posts have to be filled by open competition after the post has been advertised in a national journal. Those who are appointed are given a national training number (NTN) and this is their 'passport' to training. The actual number of NTNs is derived from complex workforce planning exercises which try to relate the number of doctors in training to the number of consultant posts becoming vacant and the predicted number of new consultant posts. More recently, there has been a greater attempt to balance numbers on a year by year basis using the number of doctors who are predicted to obtain a Certificate of Completion of Specialist Training (CCST) in the forthcoming year. Although the system works much more efficiently than the old one, there are still problems in predicting manpower precisely, and unless Trusts can be persuaded to make a better estimate of consultant appointments over the next five or six years, the workforce planning exercise will still have temporary failures. The main bottleneck has now been thrown back to the large number of SHOs who are competing for a limited number of SpR posts. However, a trainee who has an NTN is guaranteed full training in that specialty, and hopefully a consultant post at the end of the training.

A guide to specialist registrar training also provides details of special arrangements for training of doctors from overseas who may come to the UK for a limited fixed term training period or can apply for an NTN, either in competition with the UK workforce or, in more limited circumstances, using a well-defined visiting NTN. There are also rules on the availability and funding arrangements on flexible part-time training.

Anyone considering higher medical training in the UK is well advised to read *A guide to specialist registrar training* often referred to as the 'orange book'. Copies are lodged in Trust libraries and postgraduate medical centre libraries. Extra copies are available free of charge on request from the Department of Health, PO Box 410, Wetherby, West Yorkshire, LS23 7LN (www.doh.gov/uk/medicaltrainingintheuk/orangebook.htm).

College bodies involved in higher medical training

Joint Committee on Higher Medical Training

Those embarking on medical training must enrol with the Joint Committee on Higher Medical Training (JCHMT) and their application will be dealt with by the appropriate specialist advisory committee (SAC). There are 24 SACs operating under the JCHMT. The JCHMT is the overall authority acting for the Colleges of Physicians with regard to higher medical training. It in turn reports to the Specialist Training Authority (STA) and recommends to it those doctors who have completed their training and are therefore eligible for a CCST. The JCHMT functions on behalf of the three Colleges of Physicians in the United Kingdom (Edinburgh, Glasgow and London) and its responsibilities are to oversee medical training in all of the medical specialties, to approve posts and training programmes which are suitable for higher medical training and to make recommendations concerning the award of CCST. Thus, the JCHMT co-ordinates higher training in all of the medical specialties. It sets the curriculum in all specialties and is responsible for the assessment of the objectives set in the various curricula. These curricula and the training handbook can be obtained from the JCHMT office at the College (Tel: 020 7935 1174; Fax: 020 7486 4160) and can also be downloaded from the College website.

The assessment of the SpR in training is important not only for his or her development but also because of the need for the JCHMT to assure the general public that prescribed standards have been met. The assessment process (see below) is being overhauled, but, at the moment, it heavily relies on trainers' reports and the completion by trainees of the JCHMT training record, which is sent to all SpRs once they register with the JCHMT, and may be inspected at any stage during the trainees' career – in particular at the time of assessment for CCST.

Specialty advisory committees

The 24 SACs represent the Royal Colleges and the specialist associations.

Variations in the composition of the SACs are indicated in the JCHMT handbook.

Every effort is made to ensure that membership of the SACs is well balanced with adequate representation of academic medicine, regional physicians and younger consultants. Some regard for geographical spread is also desirable. The tenure of membership of SACs is normally four years and each committee elects its own chairman. SAC chairmen scrutinise the applications made by SpRs to JCHMT for recommendation of a CCST.

Enrolment into the specialist registrar grade and with JCHMT

Entry to the SpR grade is by open competition to all those with the necessary qualifications and general professional training (GPT) experience. Again, details for the procedure of the appointment to the grade are contained in the 'orange book' and the NHS Executive Good Practice Guide (*The recruitment of doctors and dentists in training*, National Health Service Executive, November 1998). On appointment, each trainee will be allotted an NTN by the postgraduate dean and subject to continuing commitment to higher training and satisfactory progression, the trainee will retain this number until the award of a CCST and, if necessary, for six months beyond. Details of appointment and enrolment in a programme will be entered by the postgraduate dean on a special form (form A) which is part of the trainee's personal record of in-training assessment (RITA) described in the 'orange book'. The JCHMT will receive a copy of this form which will serve as an adjunct to the JCHMT enrolment document and form part of the trainee's personal file. Trainees are required to enrol with the JCHMT as soon as possible after appointment to the SpR grade, and will then receive their training records after payment of a training fee. It is in the trainee's vital interest to enrol as soon as possible as their record of training depends on their enrolment (call 020 7935 1174 ext. 443).

Assessment and appraisal

Definitions of assessment and appraisal are provided in section 3 (The role of the College tutor).

Assessment
The Royal Colleges of Physicians are agreed that successful progress through a training programme should be judged on the basis of continuous assessment. Adult learning depends on a partnership between

trainer and trainee, with assessment as an aid to the achievement of goals rather than an obstacle to progress. The success of a system of continuous assessment depends on the acceptance of responsibility on the part of trainees for their own professional development. However, to meet the requirement of the specialist order, the STA must be assured that the trainee has satisfactorily completed all stages of the programme designed by the Colleges and has fulfilled all of the requirements of the curriculum. Thus, the system of assessment for the medical specialties must be of sufficient rigour and documentary validity to satisfy the STA.

Although the training programmes are for fixed periods and training is therefore predominantly 'time-based', annual assessments of 'competence' (record of in-training assessment (RITA) interviews) are required to allow progress to the next year. The panels conducting RITA interviews will, in due course, always include an external assessor, as well as a representative of the Regional Specialty Training Committee and of the postgraduate dean's department. The panel will review in detail the training record and reports from individual trainers. SpR training programmes include regular regional teaching sessions ('Calman days'), and assessment of attendance may form part of the RITA interview.

The decision reached and the documentary evidence on which it was based are entered into one of a set of standard RITA forms. There are separate forms to record:

▶ the successful completion of a year of training
▶ completion but with need for additional targeted training
▶ non-completion (implying delayed progress to the next stage of programme).

There is also a form for keeping track of those taking time out for research. Where there is need for remedial action and the trainee wishes to dispute the decision, a process of appeal is available through the postgraduate dean.

The penultimate year RITA interview which forms part of the penultimate year assessment (PYA) is particularly important, and is currently being strengthened in order to increase the rigour of assessment of competence. The precise format of this assessment is currently evolving, but may in future include a multiple-choice questionnaire and perhaps a *viva*-type interview. This is likely to be particularly the case for the general internal medicine PYA, but may not necessarily occur for the specialties.

It should be noted that a small number of medical specialties have additional exit criteria in addition to annual RITA interviews and the penultimate year assessment RITA. Trainees in haematology are required to pass the MRCPath examinations and trainees in tropical medicine must acquire the DTM&H. Although in all cases, success in these examinations is a requirement for the award of a CCST, they can be taken well in advance of completion of training so that a single failure need not necessarily delay progress or postpone a CCST award.

Appraisal

Within each year of training, there are also regular appraisal meetings between the trainee and his/her educational supervisor (or trainer – usually his/her consultant). These meetings focus on the training record, which is used to record the acquisition of experience and competence set out in the published specialty curriculum. Research achievement, teaching commitments, management training, attendance at conferences and other relevant activities are also recorded.

Award of CCSTs

The CCST is awarded to all those who complete the prescribed training programme. Responsibility for the design and immediate supervision of the programme at local level will fall mainly to the regional specialty advisors (RSA). There is some variation in the organisational structure established by postgraduate deans. Some have a single training committee in which all medical specialties are represented; others have separate specialty committees or sub-committees. All have an identified individual on whom they will depend for the many tasks associated with the management of the programmes in their specialties.

The postgraduate deans carry a responsibility for all the trainees in their regions, for their progress through the SpR grade, and for the fulfilment of the educational agreement made between the trainees, the Trusts and the specialty advisors. At the same time, the STA has a statutory responsibility for ensuring that SpR training meets the educational standards set by the Colleges and the requirements from European community legislation. The JCHMT is the College body that acts as the co-ordinating agency. The STA will seek information from the JCHMT regarding the eligibility of trainees for award of CCSTs and assurances that all of the requirements of their regulatory function have been properly met.

The role of the Colleges and the deans are complementary: both will look to the RSAs for assurances that all of the regulations attached to the running of the individual training programmes are fully complied with. RSAs will be involved in the appointment of SpRs, their annual assessments and their appeals against adverse decisions. They will also be involved in the design and supervision of training programmes. They will ensure the adequacy of appraisal systems and help with the placement of overseas doctors into training programmes. RSAs are accountable both to the deans and the Colleges. Links between RSAs and the JCHMT (as well as the appropriate SAC) are of vital importance and will assist the SACs in the evaluation and monitoring of the specialty programmes. In essence, the postgraduate dean is responsible for the local delivery of the training programme, whilst the JCHMT is responsible for ensuring that national standards are set and adhered to.

The process of application for a CCST(s) is complicated and is outlined in Figure 2. When an SpR nears completion of a training programme (usually at the expected CCST date minus six months) the relevant SAC will initiate a process of review of his or her records to satisfy itself that all of the training requirements have been met. The JCHMT will review all SAC recommendations and if it approves them, successful trainees will be told that a recommendation for the award of CCST is going forward to the STA and will be provided with the form for which to apply for it. At the same time that the STA issues this certificate, it will automatically advise the GMC that the name of the holder should be placed on the specialist register. Although there are several steps in the above process, it is streamlined as far as possible to avoid unacceptable delays. Again, it is in trainees' vital interests that all relevant documentation is completed and returned to the JCHMT as soon as possible.

In cases in which the JCHMT declines to forward a recommendation to the STA for the award of a CCST, the trainee may appeal to the JCHMT for a review of his or her training record, or for the reasons why recommendation has been withheld. If a trainee has an application for a CCST rejected, he or she is entitled to lodge a formal appeal with the STA.

No one may take up a substantive consultant post without first acquiring an entry in the specialist register; this is usually in the same specialty(s) as the intended area of practice, but is not a legal requirement. Within three months of their prospective CCST date, trainees may be interviewed for – and appointed to – consultant posts but they may not take up the post until the CCST has been awarded and entry into the specialist register made.

Flexible training

All trainees entering the SpR grade will be eligible to apply for flexible training (see section 7) but they will have to show that training on a full

At six months prior to the provisional date of award of CCST(s)
(as confirmed by the regional specialty training committee), JCHMT issues application
form(s) (separate forms for general internal medicine and specialty) for 'recommendation
of award of CCST'

↓

SpR completes form(s), which are signed by chairman/programme directors(s)
of the regional specialty training committee(s) and the postgraduate dean

↓

form(s) returned to JCHMT

↓

SAC chairman(s) scrutinises forms ± personal training record and
confirms/alters date

↓

JCHMT reviews SAC(s) assessment and recommends to STA for award of CCST(s)

↓

form for application of STA for award of CCST(s) automatically sent
to SpR, which is completed by the SpR and returned with a fee
(currently £250, paid to the STA)

↓

CCST(s) issued to SpR together with a form for entry onto the specialist register
to be returned to the STA

↓

GMC informed by STA of entry onto the specialist register

Figure 2 Process of application for CCST and entry into the Specialist Register

time basis would not be practical for well-founded individual reasons. This is a requirement of European law (EC93/16/EEC), but it is not anticipated that postgraduate deans, who will be the arbiters of practicability, will be too restricted in the interpretation of the rules in the case of either men or of women. The directive does, however, set limits on the degree of flexibility of part time training. It states that:

'part-time trainees shall meet the same requirements of full-time training, from which it will differ only in the possibility of limiting participation in medical activities to a period of at least half of that provided for full-time trainees'.

The competent authorities shall ensure that the total duration and quality of part-time trainees as specialists are not less than those of full-time trainees. This means that flexible training must involve at least five sessions per week and must include *pro rata* on-call and emergency duties. Applicants for flexible training programmes are assessed by the same criteria as those seeking full time appointments and need not declare their preference for part-time training prior to appointment.

Academic and research medicine

A commitment to academic and research medicine (see section 6) is in the long term interests of the NHS and its need remains unchallenged. A working group commissioned specifically to consider the implications of the Calman report for academic and research medicine stressed the importance of flexible interpretation of its recommendations so as to safeguard the academic sector and avoid discouragement of those contemplating entry to it. The JCHMT has a sub-committee on academic and research medicine which can advise on all aspects of training for an academic career. The timing of entry to research and academic posts is often determined by opportunity, such as the availability of a grant or the occurrence of a vacancy. For those in SpR posts, the regulations permit transfer to a research or academic appointment at any stage, subject to the agreement of the postgraduate dean and the regional specialty advisor. SpRs who are already part way through their training programme are encouraged to take time out for research while retaining their NTNs.

There is concern about doctors who are in a gap between completion of GPT and entry to the SpR grade. This is often an attractive time for trainees to undertake a period of research, although there are both advantages and disadvantages regarding the particular timing for research (see section 9). Anxiety about securing a place on the specialist training ladder must not be allowed to override an inclination towards research. The regulations clearly permit trainees in this situation to compete for SpR posts, to obtain an NTN and immediately take up a research appointment. The research should not necessarily be clinically based or necessarily be relevant to the trainees intended specialty.

Up to a year of research *may* count towards the award of a CCST, and eligibility for this should generally be agreed in advance with the JCHMT/appropriate SAC and the postgraduate dean. The JCHMT will determine on an individual basis the amount to be awarded which, to some extent, will depend on the amount of clinical work in the appropriate specialty undertaken during the research period. On completion of the research period, the trainee must decide and indicate whether they wish this period to then count towards award of a CCST.

This is important, because a retrospective decision by the SpR at the end of training, based on the availability of consultant posts, is not allowed.

Alternatively, SHOs may decide to enter research before competing for an SpR appointment. It will not be necessary to obtain prospective approval of research carried out prior to enrolment but its acceptance towards a programme of higher training remains at the discretion of the relevant SAC. On enrolment into higher training, the trainees would need to apply to the SAC giving details if he/she so wished. A later application for retrospective approval would not be accepted.

Although many trainees may wish to take only one year out for research, others may opt for a longer period, for example, to complete a higher degree. Subject to the agreement of the postgraduate dean and the regional specialty advisor and provided that an assurance of adequate monitoring of progress can be given, up to three years can be spent in research. However, it should be noted that trainees who have spent long periods in research may be asked to demonstrate their clinical competence before being asked to resume clinical duties at that particular level of training.

As described earlier, all those holding NTNs are subject to annual review. Trainees in research are required to submit annually to the postgraduate dean RITA form F, the record of out of programme experience, if they wish to retain their number. The JCHMT will receive a copy of form F and seek additional information regarding the progress of the trainee and the quality of his or her supervision. It is emphasised that the annual review system does not preclude research appointments overseas or in other UK regions, provided adequate monitoring is maintained.

Holders of university lectureships or equivalent who are pursuing higher training will require honorary SpR status and will carry NTNs. They will follow training programmes which are comparable to the NHS counterparts and movement between academic and non academic posts is encouraged. They will be required to meet the same assessment criteria for the award of a CCST, as applied to all SpRs. The work patterns for some university appointments may, however, differ significantly for those of recognised training programmes in respect of the amount of research or teaching that they involve. In such circumstances, the amount of educational credit will be determined by the JCHMT. Rigidity in the ordering of the components of a higher training programme must not be allowed to compromise opportunities for research or other academic activities. It is, however, important that the proposal for academic training agreements are confirmed in advance for the relevant SAC.

There will be some doctors in academic medicine who do not complete a clinical training programme which meets all of the requirements for the award of a CCST in one of the specialties identified in the specialist order. Their research may have taken them to a narrower specialist field in which they have great expertise and in which they wish to limit their clinical practice. For them, the route to entry in the specialist register will be through the STA on the basis of a recommendation from the JCHMT. They will not obtain a CCST, but the specialist order makes provision for such entry directly to the specialist register for doctors who have followed an unconventional career pathway. However, it is expected that the majority of doctors in academic medicine will obtain their CCST and doctors admitted under this route will be exceptional.

Overseas experience

Overseas experience is encouraged and, wherever possible, it will be given educational approval. Higher training programmes constitute a planned course with formal curriculum assessment requirements, and in order for overseas experience to be recognised for CCST purposes, it must represent an appropriate component of such a programme. Therefore, trainees contemplating going abroad should discuss their plans in advance with the programme director and the postgraduate dean, and agreement of the SAC must be sought. The SAC will assess the quality of the training and the adequacy of supervision, but will not withhold approval without good reason. Documentation attesting to satisfactory performance will be required, as in the case of the UK programmes, but conditions outlined above apply equally to those who undertake research overseas.

CHAPTER 6

Research opportunities within Calman specialist registrar training

Physicians are thinking clinicians who draw on a very strong tradition of research in the medical specialties. We know that before evidence-based medicine can be practised in a comprehensive way, much more evidence on existing care needs to be gathered by those researchers most interested in medical disorders, ie physicians. Furthermore, we look forward to new and better means to prevent, diagnose, treat and monitor the huge burden of acute and chronic disease which we manage. Indeed, in order to focus and speed progress many physicians grapple with molecular genetics, cell biology and other new technologies from which advances will spring. At the very minimum, a consultant physician needs to be 'research aware' in order to support the very important research and development function of the NHS. However, for the constitutively curious clinicians who become physicians, it has often been far more satisfying to learn about research by undertaking a dedicated period of research during specialist training. This has led many physicians, including those in district general hospitals, to maintain important and valuable programmes of research for many years. What should the pre-SpR SHO expect?

In-scheme research training

Introducing the SpR grade has been a mammoth task. The need to train physicians to a minimum level of research awareness is widely recognised, but at the time of writing the best way(s) of doing this remain uncertain. Modern medical curricula ensure that all new doctors graduate with some experience of independent study or research, but many physicians in training will have had the benefit of much more extensive experience of research during BSc or B Med Sci degrees taken as part of their undergraduate course. Indeed, some new SpRs will have spent two or three years in full time research training and will already have a higher degree (see below).

Therefore, in-scheme research training, currently loosely enshrined in most SpR programmes as a 'research half day', will need to be flexible and tailored to need. Some SpRs will need to be introduced to research, but we should remain sceptical of the current rush to introduce courses (some leading to MSc degrees) in 'research methods': these must not become deadly dull lectures on skills that SpRs will never use, given by teachers with no direct experience of clinical research. It is essential that this type of introductory training includes the expertly supervised design, execution and analysis of a small research project. Because of their strong academic background, it seems likely that the majority of medical SpRs will have more developed needs, either using their research time to prepare for 'time-out' in full-time research or, when this has been completed, to maintain and develop their research interests. What seems certain at the moment is that research training as part of the SpR grade will develop over the next few years. However, it is essential that SpRs realise that this type of training cannot be 'spoon-fed' – it requires enthusiastic, self-driven participation.

Taking time out

Despite initial concerns that SpRs would be pressured to remain 'in scheme' throughout their training, there is a widespread perception that most postgraduate teams and training scheme directors are supportive of SpRs who choose to exercise their right to take time out of the programme for externally-funded full time research. Indeed, most SACs have helped by designing curricula in which up to one year of training requirement can be substituted by suitable full time research, although despite its long-term educational value, it is appropriate that research for longer than a year does not result in any further 'rebate' from clinical training requirements.

Usually, SpRs can readily negotiate plans with their trainers to take 'time out' for a 1–2 year MD programme or a 3 year PhD training fellowship whilst funding is being sought, so that once this is available, the research period is taken at a mutually convenient stage of the SpR programme. Indeed, compared with the situation before Calman, today's research-minded SpR is in a particularly privileged position, as return to specialist clinical training at the end of the research period is guaranteed, whereas in the days when research was undertaken prior to applying for senior registrar posts, there was no such security. Furthermore, clinical work done as part of the research or ongoing sessional/on-call commitments can be considered as part of the overall SpR programme on a case-by-case basis, provided the postgraduate dean and training committee are involved prospectively; national training number (NTN)-holders taking time out from their SpR training programme should attend annual record of in-training assessment (RITA) interviews to maintain communication and to allow competion of RITA form F. Careful planning of a research period is wise, particularly for those 'bitten by the academic bug' to the extent that they decide to seek a second block of intermediate grade research training (eg clinician scientist or advanced fellowships) later in the SpR programme (see section below on academic medicine).

Difficulties with taking 'time out'

Unfortunately, no system is perfect. SpRs returning from full-time research to their training programme may not receive the plum placement on the rotation which they had hoped for, although careful prospective discussions with the director of training will help. At present, a more serious imperfection with the SpR grade is that it may be extremely difficult even for the best medical SHOs to obtain an SpR post in certain sought-after specialties, although it is hoped that this situation may improve. Some SHOs, reasoning that they have always planned to undertake a MD/PhD, and that achieving this will make them more competitive for SpR vacancies, have opted to do full time research at the end of general professional training (which comprises two year's SHO training and the MRCP).

Post-SHO, pre-SpR research needs very careful consideration. Many research leaders are still unsure of the best advice to give, because the SHO may not have had the experience to be committed to a specialty in which research is planned. A further concern is that the very brightest may be faced with five or six years' clinical training on completion of their research, making it difficult to maintain research competitiveness if they choose a career in academic medicine unless a shorter single specialty option is pursued (see relevant section). However, those SHOs fortunate enough to obtain 2–3 year research training fellowships from the Medical Research Council (MRC), Wellcome Trust or other major medical research charities, can often obtain a full NTN and a place on a training programme by applying for SpR vacancies more than 2 years before the end of the research period. If placed first at interview, the post-SHO training fellow can defer entry to the SpR training programme, secure in the knowledge that he/she now has an NTN (temporarily 'inactive'), and the programme is allowed to appoint the second-placed candidate to an extra NTN, subject to the postgraduate dean's approval. Everyone benefits from this strategy.

However, most SHOs doing pre-SpR research do not have such 'blue chip' funding (see below) and will not qualify for a tightly-regulated arrangement, which is intended to foster a small number of future academic leaders. It is therefore particularly important that the research is well planned and likely to yield the thesis and publications that will prove attractive to SPR selection panels. Many SHOs considering such pre-SpR research should also think carefully about the alternative of strengthening the quality of their experience at SHO level and/or obtaining up to one year of locum appointment training (LAT) experience in their preferred specialty, as both strategies could prove equally attractive to SpR appointment committees. Careful discussion with mentors is essential. Research is not something to do because there seems to be no other way forward.

Funding and quality of research

Time out in research requires external funding which, at a minimum, should cover the SpR's salary and national insurance/pension costs etc. The MRC, Wellcome Trust and other major medical research charities only have funds to support the highest quality research. Such 'blue chip' awards must be planned for carefully, as the need for peer review of applications means that the lead-in time may be 9–12 months, because the quality of the project is even more critical than the quality of the candidate and the host unit, which must be high. Although physicians in training obtain around two thirds of the 120–140 research training awards available nationally each year, it should be obvious that not all research-minded medical SpRs can expect to obtain such awards. Much valuable research is supported by smaller local charities, endowment funds and the pharmaceutical industry. Nevertheless, before accepting the offer of a research post from a respected senior colleague, an SpR should clarify the source of the funding and consider whether the unit concerned has a track record of high quality research and a stimulating inter-disciplinary environment; talking to current and former research fellows is essential. If the SpR finds an enthusiastic, productive and mutually supportive research unit then it would be unwise to overlook any forthcoming offer unless they have serious academic intentions. Indeed, such sources can provide a young researcher with a spring board from which to obtain a prestigious fellowship.

A 1st class or 2:1 BSc/B Med Sci is not essential to obtain a 'blue chip' award, as the Wellcome Trust have a one year 'entry level' scheme for those without an 'intercalated' degree so that after acquiring some experience of research the award holder can then compete for a substantive training fellowship in which to complete a PhD thesis. Furthermore, while the era when having a PhD might adversely influence a consultant appointments committee has (probably!) passed, many very able SpRs prefer not to commit themselves to a three year PhD programme, opting for a shorter period leading to an MD thesis. Funding which is not 'blue chip' could provide just the opportunity required, but it is important to remember that most universities have recently tightened regulations for MD degrees so that a supervised period after prospective registration is essential, although this usually spans only one year. Therefore, the length of time for which a research salary can be guaranteed is important if a higher degree is sought. Generally speaking, a higher degree is a highly desirable outcome of a dedicated period of research since it provides incontrovertible evidence of a productive and scholarly experience. However, the message should be clear: obtaining a first-class research training fellowship leading to a PhD is not the only way to access a rewarding period in full-time research.

Conclusions

Research is an integral part of a physician's job and most consultants who have undertaken full time research value the experience, and many continue to make important contributions throughout their career. Introduction of the SpR grade may have freed a small number of reluctant trainees from the yoke of apparently compulsory research, but it has also enhanced the attractiveness of full time research as this can be undertaken in a secure, planned manner mid-way through a clinical training scheme. Furthermore, as SpR curricula develop, in-scheme research training will be increasingly valuable, provided that it is tailored to need. However, physicians in training need to exercise their critical faculties in choosing the research opportunity which best suits their plans and aspirations. Obtaining expert advice is essential but this is freely available from physicians working in research, as well as from trainers, specialist societies, funding bodies and the postgraduate dean. There has never been a more exciting time at which to undertake medical research – try it and see.

CHAPTER 7

Flexible training

The Royal College of Physicians is strongly committed to flexible training and has a specific officer with particular responsibility for flexible training and flexible working. The demography of the medical workforce is changing rapidly and the National Health Service Executive recognises that it is vital to provide as many opportunities as possible for part-time training. Flexible training and working in medicine is no longer a rarity. Currently 6 per cent of SpRs in medicine train flexibly. Flexible training can be undertaken by any grade of hospital physician and in any sub-specialty. At present, 98 per cent of flexible trainees are women with children who choose to undertake part of their training part-time because of family commitments. However, the flexible training option is open to any trainee provided they can show that to train on a full time basis would not be practical for well-founded individual reasons. This is a requirement of European law (EC93/16/EEC). The scheme is administered by the postgraduate deans and each region has an associate dean for flexible training. Although the deaneries are relaxed in their interpretation of eligibility, they are bound by the European directive which sets limits on the degree of flexibility, stating:

'part-time training shall meet the same requirements of full-time training from which it will differ only in the possibility of limiting participation in medical activities to a period of at least half of that provided for full-time trainees'.

This means that flexible training must involve at least five sessions per week and must include pro-rata on-call and emergency duties. No-one should be deterred from a career in any branch of hospital medicine simply because they want the option of spending more time outside the hospital during their training. Combining work and family life is difficult for many trainees, and flexible training is a realistic and accessible solution. However, it is important to remember that currently the duration of training is increased on a pro-rata basis and the salary decreased similarly. Therefore, most flexible trainees working six four-hour sessions per week take roughly twice as long to train and receive half the salary during this period. The drop-out rate is very low and most doctors choosing this pattern of training will eventually leave for academic or consultant posts, or complete their training on a full-time basis.

The quality of training is at least as good as for full-time posts. The entry to each grade requires the same standard as for a full-time trainee, and flexible trainees are neither advantaged or disadvantaged with respect to their region's varied training opportunities.

Plenty of time is required for posts to be set up, so if a trainee is planning a family or thinks that he or she may have other well-founded reasons for training flexibly, early discussion should take place with the associate dean for flexible training in the region. It is possible to organise flexible training at SpR, SHO or pre-registration level, but most flexible trainees are SpRs.

It is the associate dean for flexible training in each region who decides on eligibility. Educational approval and funding for pre-registration posts is agreed with the local university.

At SHO level, flexible training posts may be sharing of an established post, or one of the new permanent part-time training posts established mainly in the London region. The number of sessions per week is usually between five and seven. When a new supernumerary post is created by the Associate Dean for flexible training, additional on-call is required on a pro-rata basis to full-timers, and each hospital on the rotation will have to pay ADHs. It is important that this is discussed explicitly with the supervisor, as it takes time and negotiation to find funding. When planning a flexible training post, Individual Specialty Forms (ISFs) can be obtained from the manager of General Professional Training (GPT) at the College. In addition to a completed ISF and job description, the GPT office will require a copy of the candidate's CV and a commencement date for the post. On receipt of the completed paperwork, the GPT office and the appropriate regional advisor of the Royal College of Physicians will assess the post for educational approval. Audit and formal education should be included in the timetable as well as the total number of sessions to be worked. This procedure will have to be repeated for each different post occupied during the flexible training programme.

At SpR level, candidates for flexible training programmes are assessed by the same criteria as those seeking full time appointments. All advertisements for SpR posts will indicate that they are open to full-time and part-time applicants on a competitive basis. Applicants are not required to declare their intention to work part-time for any part of the programme prior to appointment; nor are appointments committees entitled to enquire. Interviews are conducted with other full-time prospective SpRs and all candidates are graded on merit alone. It is worth while discussing an application with the associate dean in advance of the interview since some funding preparations can then be made prior to possible appointment. In addition, the postgraduate dean may issue an extra NTN after consultation with the specialty lead dean. At SpR level, liaison with the JCHMT office at the College is required (see chapter 5). The JCHMT programmes should now be sufficiently flexible (in the larger specialties) to enable trainees to change from whole-time to part-time training without the need to submit a revised programme of training and curriculum vitae. The local programme director/supervisor will be able to advise. In the event that a revision to the training programme is required, the programme director should speak to the JCHMT office to obtain form A (amendment to the agreed programme) and form B (application for approval of a new training slot).

If possible, flexible trainees are encouraged by the deanery to job-share, but currently over 90 per cent are supernumerary in the medical specialties. Job-sharing is a more likely option in specialties with a high proportion of flexible trainees. The postgraduate deans hold the budget for the basic salary costs of flexible trainees, but the responsibility for the payment of ADHs rests with the employing trust. For supernumerary posts, as well as funding, an educational programme will need to be arranged including details of hospital rotations and on-call commitments. This will need to be planned and agreed between the candidate, the programme director, specialist training committee (STC) chair and regional adviser. In some regions, within each STC there is now a named lead consultant with a special interest in flexible training. Trainees can transfer from full-time to part-time, or from part-time to full-time at SpR level by arrangement with their programme director and the flexible training office of the deanery. Increasingly, there are also opportunities in some regions for part-time academic posts, and trainees should again approach their associate dean. Study leave entitlement (and in some regions funding) is identical for flexible and full-time trainees, and is not currently on a pro-rata basis.

Candidates should not be put off by the apparent complexity of the application procedure. Once he or she has approached the associate dean for flexible training, most of the organisation occurs painlessly and automatically.

Anyone considering flexible training within the next year should approach their associate dean for flexible training. This can be in confidence, if necessary. Their name and address can be found on the website given at the end of this section.

Further information can be obtained from

Appendix 7, *GPT Guide for Trainees and Trainers*. Available from the College
website: http://www.rcplondon.ac.uk/pubs/handbook/gpt/gpt_handbook_app7.htm
North Thames website: http://www.nthames-health.tpmde.ac.uk/flexible/

CHAPTER 8

Management training

The role of doctors in management positions throughout the NHS has developed considerably over the last ten years. Once regarded as an occupation for the failed clinician or the eccentric, the clinician with well developed management and leadership skills is now regarded as a crucial player in the organisation – both at local and at national levels.

Management skills, however, cannot be developed a couple of days prior to the consultant interview, along with some earnest brushing up on audit techniques and clinical governance. In today's healthcare, potential employers are seeking individuals who have cultivated their management and leadership skills, have led and managed projects, managed teams and can demonstrate a wide range of interpersonal and technological skills.

Medical schools are increasingly including management as part of their curricula; indeed some are offering intercalated degree courses in management studies. The newly appointed consultant without manage-ment experience may well find him or herself outsmarted by junior staff in these areas. It makes sense to develop management and leadership skills throughout the specialist registrar years so that by consultant stage they are well developed and the individual is confident and comfortable with management matters.

All clinical roles, regardless of specialty, embrace management to some extent. All clinicians in today's healthcare, work as part of multi-disciplinary teams in which highly tuned skills are needed to work effectively. Some clinicians may wish to develop their management skills still further and take on a specific role within their organisations – clinical directors head up clinical specialties and are responsible for the smooth running of the service, its quality and the resources of the directorate. Clinical directors play both a managerial and a strategic role in the organisation, in addition to their clinical roles.

Others may wish to pursue a role as medical director, the key responsibility for the quality of clinical care for the entire organisation, sitting on the Trust Board. These individuals typically spend at least 50 per cent of their working time on management matters.

Other management roles include leading clinical risk management teams and clinical audit teams, and working on projects to implement clinical guidelines.

Training for management roles

Any programme of management development for clinicians, regardless of the stage of their career, must combine the following elements:

- ▶ Interpersonal skills, influencing and leadership skills
- ▶ Formal, taught programmes of learning or management systems and processes
- ▶ Experience – responsibility for management projects, shadowing chief executives, directors of human resource management, finance managers and other key managerial roles.

Doctors in training should take advantage of any courses or programmes offered to them, either by their Trust or perhaps on a regional basis. They should also seek out their own management development programmes and pursue these. They should make full use of the expertise available to them within their organisation, by asking managerial and senior clinical colleagues for help and for opportunities to run projects and shadow appropriate colleagues. The British Association of Medical Managers (www.bamm.co.uk) runs a number of programmes and can provide advice and information to doctors wishing to develop management skills.

Investment in these activities early on in a clinical career will pay enormous dividends later on. The consultant role is essentially a managerial one – leading a team which will deliver a service. Without an active management development programme at SpR level, newly appointed consultants find themselves poorly equipped to do the job to which they have been appointed. This can be a depressing, demoralising experience and one which doctors in training are well advised to avoid.

Advice on applying for consultant appointments

Members often raise questions about the 'fairness' of advisory appointments committees (AACs) for NHS consultant posts. It is therefore appropriate to include a personal view on a sensible approach to the ordeal of applying for a permanent job.

The job description for a consultant post will usually have been carefully drawn up to suit the needs of the department concerned, but is also influenced by other senior hospital staff and, increasingly, by managers. So statements such as 'a special interest would be an advantage' require further informal investigation. The department might have clear ideas as to what that special interest should be but have been prevented from making the job description too specific; similarly, the job description may have been designed to suit a candidate known to other members of the department, though this may not be immediately obvious. Careful, even probing, enquiries may be needed to establish how the candidate's prospective colleagues and administrators envisage his or her pattern of work and interests, which avoids this discovery being made at a wasted interview and guards against appointment to a job that is not as the candidate had expected it. A visit to the district to make tactful enquiries is an important initial mutual assessment between applicant and potential colleagues, and, if the candidate knows of a forthcoming vacancy, it may be worthwhile suggesting such a visit several months before the post is advertised. One of these visits should include discussion with the trust medical director or chief executive about the trust's plans, the commissioners' aims and any effects of local financial pressure and future service developments. At this stage, it is also important to clarify junior staff allocation, their hours of work, split rotas etc.

An application should always be accompanied by a clear statement of why the candidate wants the job, what he or she hopes to contribute to the hospital, and should stress the appropriateness of his or her qualifications and experience. Weighting of a *curriculum vitae* is entirely appropriate – all of one's training will not be equally applicable to the rest of one's professional life; for example, research experience would probably need different emphasis in applications for a teaching hospital and a district general hospital post. It is essential, however, for a candidate to be scrupulously honest in all of his or her statements. Word processors are invaluable!

During the period after applying, most appropriately after being short-listed, it is important to give a candidate and his or her future colleagues and administrators the opportunity of getting to know each other, at least superficially. The appointment of a close colleague is one of the most important professional decisions of a lifetime and can be likened to a marriage. It is not in the interests of either party to appoint an incompatible colleague and, while no member of the committee has a veto, a statement by the department representative that a particular candidate would be difficult to work with would be a high hurdle to jump at the interview. In this context the question of favouring a local or known candidate can be put in perspective. 'The devil you know' is a powerful argument. In spite of this, it is rare for an AAC's decision to be a foregone conclusion, particularly if the job has attracted a good field. It is unwise to withdraw because there is a strong local candidate: in the first place, all is not always as it appears from outside; second, strong support in favour of a candidate from an individual member of the committee who knows him or her (and will have declared this) is unlikely to have a major effect on the outcome; finally, the feared rival candidate may withdraw or be appointed elsewhere before the interview.

Locum consultant posts are sometimes advertised 'pending a substantive appointment'. The value of taking such a post is difficult to assess, and close discussion with mentors is advisable. The first months of working as a consultant, even, and perhaps especially, in a locum capacity, are trying times and it may be difficult to make the desired impression. Nevertheless, there is no doubt that in some substantive appointments, good performance in a preceding locum appointment is a clinching factor. It is vital to discuss such a locum consultant appointment with the chairman of one's regional specialty training committee to ensure smooth passage back to a training programme in the event of not being appointed to the substantive post. Furthermore, if a consultant oversees the locum post, up to three months of accreditation may be obtained towards a CCST.

If, after enquiries, the candidate decides that he or she really wants the post and appears to be appropriately qualified, an examination of personal strengths and weaknesses is clearly necessary (particularly those that were inappropriately included or omitted from the application). The candidate will need to be prepared to defend (or acknowledge and explain) the latter, preferably with suggestions as to how they might be remedied before taking up the appointment.

At the interview, it is rarely the *curriculum vitae* that decides the recommendation of the AAC. Honesty and openness are important – probing questions are usually probing for a good reason, and it is unusual for the AAC to be deceived. Personality is an important consideration but a candidate will not be marked down for an expected degree of nervousness. Clear statements as to aims and ambitions in the new post are valuable – most AACs wish to feel that a candidate knows where they are going, and that they will pay due attention to the needs and aspirations of future colleagues.

Given that more than one candidate with appropriate qualifications and experience appears at the interview, factors other than those on the application form will probably decide the outcome. To complain, 'I was better qualified for the job' (than the person appointed) is irrelevant; if the appointed candidate was less qualified on his *curriculum vitae* it is likely that he or she displayed other qualities which another candidate either lacked or did not bring out at that interview.

It is rare for the recommendation of an AAC to be unfair; it is more usual for apparent unfairness to be due to the AAC having given weight to less obvious attributes of the candidates. The role of the College's representatives on the AAC is outlined in Chapter 10.

If a candidate has serious reservations about the suitability of a post, they should bear in mind the fact that it is quite acceptable to withdraw an application right up to the moment of the interview. This is much better than being offered the post at the end of interview and vacillating or, even worse, turning it down a few days later. A lot of effort goes into the selection procedure at interview, and word will spread if a candidate changes his or her mind after interview. Do your homework and make your decision in advance!

CHAPTER 10

Consultant appointments committees

Appointment of a consultant in the NHS follows a set procedure: the appointment must be advertised, an advisory appointments committee (AAC) must be convened, an interview held and the person selected by the committee recommended to the employing trust. In the case of academic appointments (eg senior lecturers), the College is usually, but not obligatorily, invited to send a representative to the appointments committee.

Before a post can be advertised, several steps must be taken. The hospital trust decides the nature of the appointment it would like to see made. No matter whether it is a new post or a replacement, there may be conflicting views on its character and on details of the job description. Local medical opinion is likely to predominate in making the decisions, but the administration will also have substantial input.

When the appropriate authority has decided what it requires, but before the post can be advertised, the job description is submitted for approval by the College regional adviser, who may ask that certain aspects be changed or, rarely, even disallow the appointment altogether. The regional adviser may take advice concerning a proposed appointment from the regional specialty adviser and/or the chairman or secretary of the College specialty committee. College committees in the various specialties have drawn up guidelines to help regional advisers assess the suitability of an appointment, giving general guidance as to the facilities and resources required for a consultant appointment in that specialty. These guidelines have been scrutinised by the Council of the College to make sure that they are in harmony with each other and that, while insisting on essential requirements, they do not demand so much that the post becomes impossibly expensive.

When its description has been approved, the post is advertised in the medical press. A consultant AAC for that post is set up. Its composition is determined by statute and includes representatives from the hospital in which the appointment is to be made with at least one colleague from the same specialty, a university representative and a College representative (CR). The CR, who must come from outside the NHS region concerned, is almost invariably a fairly senior Fellow of the College. Most Fellows are regarded as suitable to represent the College on consultant AACs but some may be less so, perhaps because of their narrow field of interest or because they are known to have many other commitments. The College tries to ensure that a wide variety of Fellows represents it on these important committees.

Methods of short-listing vary; the CR should be fully involved in this process. The most common method is for each member of the committee to judge the candidates and then four or five are invited for interview.

The CR is a full member of the AAC, with neither more nor less power than the others, and is charged by the College with seeing that the selected candidate is adequately trained for the appointment. Interview candidates must be on, or eligible to be on, the specialist register, usually by virtue of either holding a CCST, or of being within three months of its recommended award. Although it is not a statutory requirement, the College recommends that the specialty on the register is appropriate to the post. For instance, in the case of appointment of a cardiologist with a commitment to unselected medical 'take', it is strongly recommended that the appointed doctor holds CCSTs in both cardiology and general internal medicine. If a candidate is appropriate for the appointment but lacks some limited aspect of training, for example proficiency in a technique, the AAC may recommend that he or she undertakes further training for a few weeks or months before taking up the appointment. The recommendation of the AAC is usually announced to the candidates at the end of the meeting.

The CR is free to question applicants on all aspects of their application, not merely the adequacy or otherwise of their specialist experience. The CR is asked by the College to emphasise its interest in encouraging research and to bring out a candidate's research contributions. The CR has a vote in the committee's decision but does not have a veto; if not satisfied about a selection, the CR may report to the College and even, in exceptional circumstances, ask the College to take up the objections with the employing authority.

The number and quality of applicants for consultant appointments vary greatly. Some specialties are less popular than others and may attract few and poor applications; for this reason, occasionally no appointment is made. In other specialties the competition is intense and 10–20 high-class applications may be received.

CHAPTER 11

Advice for doctors from overseas

The UK has long welcomed doctors from many other nations who come to this country for postgraduate training. Some come for a few weeks or months to learn a particular technique or skill, or to participate in a formal exchange programme, while others may come for several years to undertake general professional or specialist training. Some stay for many years and build successful careers here – approximately 20 per cent of doctors on the UK medical register qualified outside the UK/EU. The College recognises that overseas doctors contribute a great deal to the medical profession in the UK both while here and when they return to their home countries.

This section aims to provide some general advice for overseas doctors who are interested in training in the UK and also aims to provide a pointer to sources of information, advice and support.

The European Union

Doctors who are citizens of the European Union or European Economic Area (EU/EEA)[1] and who hold an EU/EEA medical qualification or are fully registered in an EU/EEA member state are treated for immigration and medical registration purposes as UK citizens. Advice about the recognition of postgraduate training and specialist qualifications is available from the College's General Professional Training Office (GPT Enquiries) or from the Joint Committee on Higher Medical Training (JCHMT) (Specialist Training/Specialist Registration enquiries)

Who can come to the UK for training?

For doctors who have no rights of indefinite leave to remain in the EU/EEA, the position is rather more complicated. In order to be able to practise in the UK there are a number of hurdles which need to be negotiated.

---

[1] EU Member States: Austria, Belgium, Denmark, Finland, France, Germany, Greece, Italy, Liechtenstein, Luxembourg, Netherlands, Portugal, Republic of Ireland, Spain, Sweden, UK. EEA Member States: Iceland, Norway.

Anyone whose qualifications are recognised by the World Health Organisation (WHO) is entitled to apply for registration in the UK. Anyone with a qualification not recognised by the WHO may apply to have his or her qualification recognised. Overseas doctors will also be expected to have completed an acceptable internship of at least twelve months duration.

Clinical attachments

Clinical attachments are informal arrangements whereby overseas doctors may observe clinical work in a UK hospital. They do not require GMC registration and those undertaking them do not need to take the Professional and Linguistic Assessment Board (PLAB) test.

The PLAB test

Medical graduates from outside the EU must take the PLAB test before they can be granted registration. The test is administered by the GMC and in addition to being available in London, Edinburgh and Glasgow can now also be taken at the following overseas centres:

Bangladesh:	Dhaka
Egypt:	Cairo
India:	Calcutta
	Chennai
	Delhi
	Mumbai
Pakistan:	Islamabad
	Karachi
Sri Lanka:	Colombo

PLAB exemption

The GMC is able to consider certain overseas doctors for exemption from the PLAB test. The grounds on which applications for exemption may be considered are: seniority; appointment to a Type I specialist training post; completion of basic specialist training and eligibility for entry at the top of the specialist register.

The IELTS test

All doctors from outside the EU/EEA must score satisfactorily in the International English Language Testing System (IELTS) test before they can be granted registration. This applies to applicants for all forms of registration regardless of their mother tongue. Information on IELTS and test centres in the UK and overseas is available from the British Council.

Limited registration

Most overseas doctors being granted initial UK registration will be given limited registration. Limited registration is only granted for employment that is supervised and in an educationally approved training post at Senior House Officer or Specialist Registrar grades. Holders of limited registration may not take consultant or locum posts.

Full registration

Doctors who have held limited registration for a minimum of two years may apply to the GMC for full registration. The GMC will take up references from consultants who have supervised the applicant before making a decision on the application.

Under the provisions of the Medical Act (1983) some overseas doctors are entitled to full registration by virtue of their primary medical qualification. Applicants for full registration must take the IELTS test, either in the UK or at one of the following overseas centres:

Australia
University of Newcastle, New South Wales
University of New South Wales
University of Sydney
University of Queensland
University of Adelaide
Flinders University of South Australia
University of Tasmania
University of Melbourne
Monash University
University of Western Australia

Hong Kong
University of Hong Kong
Chinese University of Hong Kong

Malaysia
University of Malaya, Kuala Lumpur

New Zealand
University of Auckland

University of Otago
University of New Zealand

Singapore
National University of Singapore
University of Singapore

South Africa
University of Cape Town
University of Natal
University of the Orange Free State
University of Pretoria
University of Stellenbosch
University of Witwatersrand

West Indies
University of the West Indies

Posts

All posts in the training grades are advertised in the medical press and subject to competitive interview. There are no training posts in the UK set aside specifically for overseas doctors. Competition for training posts in all grades is very intense and it is important that overseas doctors seek advice on CV preparation, and the interview and appointment process.

Immigration

Many overseas doctors are entitled to UK residence by virtue of ancestry, marriage or residence. Others are able to take advantage of the provisions for work-permit free training. Doctors entering the UK for SHO and SpR posts may be granted an initial period of three years permit free training. With the support of their postgraduate deans, SHOs may then be granted a one year extension while SpRs may apply for extensions until they become eligible for a CCST.

Information and advice

This has been a brief overview of some of the major issues facing overseas doctors wishing to train in the UK.

Overseas doctors wishing to train in the UK should be aware that competition for training places, particularly at the level of specialist training can be very intense. Before making a decision to come to the UK all doctors are urged to seek advice about the situation in the specialty in which they wish to train.

A great deal of advice is available, and the organisations listed below are just some of those able to help.

The British Council, which has offices throughout the world, is the best source of local information for those outside the UK, while the National Advice Centre for Postgraduate Medical Education publishes a series of highly informative leaflets which are available both on paper and through its website.

International Office
Royal College of Physicians
11 St Andrews Place
London
NW1 4LE
Tel: + 44 20 7935 1174 ext 319
Fax: + 44 20 7486 4034
E-mail: international@rcplondon.ac.uk
Website: http://www.rcplondon.ac.uk

General Medical Council
178 Great Portland Street
London
W1W 5JE
Tel: + 44 20 7580 7642
Fax: + 44 20 7915 3641
Website: www.gmc-uk.org

British Council
Bridgewater House
58 Whitworth Street
Manchester
M1 6BB
Tel: + 44 161 957 7474
Fax: + 44 161 957 7029
Website: www.britcoun.org.uk

National Advice Centre for Postgraduate Medical Education
STIU, 3rd Floor
British Council
Medlock Street
Manchester
M15 4AA
Tel: + 44 161 957 7218
Website: www.britcoun.org/health/nacpme

Department for Education and Employment
Overseas Labour Service
West 5, Moorfoot
Sheffield
S1 4PQ
Tel: + 44 114 259 4071
Fax: + 44 114 259 3707
Website: www.dfee.gov.uk

Immigration and Nationality Directorate
Home Office
Lunar House
40 Wellesley Road
Croydon
CR9 2BY
Tel: + 44 20 8686 0688
Website: www.homeoffice.gov.uk

CHAPTER 12

The Trainees Committee

History and role

Trainee physicians have at times considered the activities of the Royal College of Physicians to be somewhat removed from the grass-roots of training to be a physician. With this in mind, the Trainees Committee was established in 1996, principally to address the needs of the ever-increasing 'lost tribe' of medical SHOs. Consequently, the committee's work initially focused on issues predominantly related to the MRCP exam. During the following three years, the committee's remit broadened to include matters pertaining to the newly-created Calman SpR grade, and now represents the views of all medical trainees from pre-MRCP SHOs through to senior SpRs. Approximately 30 trainees elected regionally to represent England, Wales and Northern Ireland attend four meetings annually, together with the College President, Registrar, Director of Training (Linacre Fellow), SpR Advisor and other College officers whose posts relate to training. Trainees Committee representatives also have the opportunity to air their views on College Council, College boards, the JCHMT and those College working parties related to training issues. Thus, the committee acts as a conduit between junior physicians and the governing body of the RCP. In addition, the Trainees Committee is the main point of reference at the RCP for associate College tutors, providing them with regular updates of College matters in a dedicated newsletter and organising the annual Associate College Tutor's Day at the Royal College of Physicians.

Projects to date

The Trainees Committee's work to date has centred largely on SHO issues, such as helping to establish the core curriculum and the personal training record for SHOs, defining guidelines for effective handover on-call and also guidelines on what to expect from MRCP Part II clinical courses. The committee has also been involved in the development of associate RCP membership, a scheme designed to encourage pre-MRCP trainees to be part of the RCP at a subsidised fee. In addition, we continue to audit MRCP

Part II clinical courses and the committee's publicity officers are involved in updating the College website. In the future we hope to contribute to the establishment of a careers advice service for trainees based at the RCP and to provide guidelines on appraisal for trainees.

Summary

The Trainees Committee is a relatively newly established group which continues to evolve to meet the needs of all trainee physicians. Vacancies on the committee arise annually and elections of candidates who have been proposed by a RCP Collegiate member (eg College or Associate College Tutor) are held by regional mailings. Trainees who are prepared to share their views yet listen to those of others, who would value some experience of learning how to effect change, and who feel they could make the necessary time commitment are urged to join. The committee can be contacted directly by email (Trainees.Committee@rcplondon.ac.uk) and regular updates of committee activities can be found via the College website (www.rcplondon.ac.uk/professional/gpt_tc.htm).

Part 2 Individual specialties

See end of each section for addresses of specialty societies and further information

Academic medicine
Accident & emergency medicine
Cardiology
Clinical genetics
Clinical neurophysiology
Clinical pharmacology & therapeutics
Dermatology
Endocrinology and diabetes mellitus
Gastroenterology
General internal medicine
Genitourinary medicine
Geriatric medicine
Haematology
Immunology
Infectious diseases and tropical medicine
Intensive care medicine
Medical oncology
Neurology
Nuclear medicine
Occupational medicine
Palliative medicine
Pharmaceutical medicine
Public health medicine
Rehabilitation medicine
Renal medicine
Respiratory medicine
Rheumatology

Academic medicine

Whilst not a medical specialty in itself, academic medicine can form an integral part of any individual specialty. Academic medicine offers the opportunity to be involved in the cutting edge of medical research, medical education and clinical care.

The consultant's job

Academic medicine encompasses many different types of career, from that of a typical clinical academic member of staff in an undergraduate medical school or postgraduate school, to that of a senior researcher in an MRC unit or charitably funded institution. Most posts in undergraduate medical schools will have a broad portfolio that can include responsibility for undergraduate medical education and significant clinical responsibility. The clinical work of an academic physician will usually reflect a combination of the research interests of the individual concerned and their requirement for access to patients for teaching. A clinical academic career can be entirely focused on research, particularly if personal support is obtained through the MRC, Wellcome Trust and other research career support schemes, or via appointment to a position in a research unit or institution. The type of research performed by a clinical academic can vary widely from very basic science, eg cell and molecular biology, to more conventional patient-oriented clinical investigation, or to social sciences and health services research.

Training requirements

From the description of the consultant's job, it will be appreciated that there are many different routes and methods of training for academic medicine. As most academic posts include consultant level clinical responsibility, it is usual to obtain the appropriate general professional and then specialist training for your chosen field of interest. A few individuals choose a less clearly defined route and opt for limited clinical accreditation (eg in a very specialist field) or rarely some pursue an entirely research driven training and thereby opt not to practice clinical medicine at consultant level. At present there is no defined or proscribed training for a clinical academic, although the RCP is seeking to develop improved guidelines and training schemes.

Training in research is clearly a key component of becoming a clinical academic and it is important to receive an in depth training in your chosen 'scientific' area of interest in addition to obtaining a thorough training in scientific approaches and methodology. This can be performed either before higher medical training or during the Specialist Registrar grade; award of a higher degree should be the goal in this stage of training for academic medicine. Further information can be found in part one of this book in chapter 6: *Research opportunities within Calman specialist registrar training.*

The next step involves the development of an independent research profile and is, for obvious reasons, the most difficult to achieve. MRC clinician scientist awards or Wellcome Trust intermediate fellowships offer a major opportunity to fund this period and are highly prestigious. Another alternative is to obtain a post as a clinical lecturer in an academic department. Either route is associated with completing clinical training, but this takes careful planning in consultation with your regional speciality advisor, training programme director, postgraduate dean and funding organisation. When relevant this stage can include a period of research in another institution or abroad to acquire new research techniques and to help advance your research activity and profile.

Career prospects

There are several factors driving a gradual expansion of clinical academic posts in the UK. All medical schools are now assessed on a regular basis for their research and teaching excellence. This has led to an increasing need for well-trained, research-active clinical academic staff that can also contribute to teaching. The government has recently announced a major expansion of medical student numbers in the UK and this will lead to further expansion of clinical academic posts. There has also been an increase in the number of senior fellowships and other types or personal support from the MRC and other major funding organisations. The current prospects for a successful career in academic medicine are therefore extremely good. Those choosing an entirely research based career via research institutions and units should be aware that this can be very competitive and only the very best researchers will continue to be funded long term. However this has always been the case and the rewards of working in such a professional research environment can be very high.

Further information

Useful websites:
Medical Research Council: www.mrc.ac.uk
Wellcome Trust: www.wellcome.ac.uk

Accident & emergency medicine

It is thirty years since casualty departments became accident & emergency (A & E) departments and some of them are now departments of emergency medicine. A & E specialists are the generalists of hospital practice and undertake an increasingly important role at the interface with the community. There is an active specialty association, the British Association for Accident & Emergency Medicine, and the academic, research and training aspects are within the remit of the Intercollegiate Faculty of Accident & Emergency Medicine, a joint Faculty of the Royal Colleges of Physicians, Surgeons and Anaesthetists.

The consultant's job

The consultant workload involves an immense spectrum of clinical problems but resuscitation of the acutely ill and injured always takes priority. The A & E consultant is responsible for ensuring that the rising number of emergency admissions are appropriately assessed and receive relevant initial investigation and management before they are transferred for inpatient care. The working day is relatively unstructured because of the essential requirement to be able to respond without warning to unexpected and unpredictable events. Nonetheless, many A & E departments run regular review clinics and an increasing number have an observation ward for the management of patients who require a brief period of inpatient management, eg having taken an overdose or suffered a moderately severe head injury. Quality control and audit are an important part of the daily routine and many consultants have special clinical interests, such as paediatric medicine, intensive care or sports medicine, and areas of specific responsibility such as pre-hospital care and disaster planning.

The leadership attributes required of a successful A & E consultant are many but include especially the ability to organise and work as part of a multi-disciplinary team. Diplomacy and tact are essential to communicate and liaise effectively with the most difficult of colleagues and patients, in addition to adaptability, flexibility and managerial and clinical skills. There must also be a commitment and ability to teach and to train because the A & E department is one of the best learning environments for senior house officers and medical students.

Training requirements

The training programme lasts for five years and normally involves rotation between two or three hospitals in a given region. Those entering higher specialist training will have undertaken a minimum of two years of general professional training, preferably including at least one year of A & E experience, before obtaining an appropriate higher qualification. Other relevant GPT experience includes general medicine, paediatrics, anaesthetics and orthopaedics. Higher qualifications acceptable for entry into specialist registrar training include the MRCP(UK/I), the new MRCS in Surgery in General (or the preceding FRCS), Part 2 of the new FRCA examination and the MRCS in A & E (a specialty exam available through the Royal College of Surgeons of Edinburgh).

During the early years of training, trainees are required to undertake full-time attachments of at least three months in the 'core' specialties of general medicine, anaesthetics (with ICU experience), general paediatrics, orthopaedic trauma and surgical specialties (including neurosurgery and plastic surgery), unless they have previously obtained the relevant experience during GPT. Other valuable secondments include elderly care medicine, general practice and psychiatry. A maximum of one year of relevant research can be included within the training programme. Following satisfactory completion of the fourth year of training, trainees are required to pass the specialty examination of the Faculty of Accident & Emergency Medicine (FFAEM) in order to be eligible for the award of their CCST.

Career prospects

Career prospects are good for specialist registrars currently entering a training programme but workforce planning may require some reduction in the number of available posts. There are now more than 500 A & E consultants in the UK and there will be further significant increase in this number during the next decade. It is possible that some smaller hospitals may cease to offer a full A & E service but the many departments that remain will become busier and will need to increase their consultant establishment. A & E medicine is likely to remain a consultant-led service for the foreseeable future but there is already pressure in the largest departments for consultant presence to extend into the evenings and weekends. This can be achieved on a sessional basis and this means that flexible working, job sharing and part-time working at consultant level are more feasible than in some other acute clinical specialties.

A & E medicine offers an enormously diverse and challenging career for those who wish to practise acute medicine within a hospital setting. It seems inevitable that its boundaries will have been considerably extended before the next edition of this guide is published.

Further information

The Registrar
Faculty of Accident and Emergency Medicine
35–43 Lincoln's Inn Fields
London WC2A 3PN
Tel: 020 7405 7071
Fax: 020 7405 0318
E-mail: faem@compuserve.com
Website: www.faem.org.uk

The Secretary
The British Association for Accident & Emergency Medicine
35–43 Lincoln's Inn Fields
London WC2A 3PN
Tel: 020 7831 9405
Fax: 020 7405 0318
E-mail: baem1@compuserve.com
Website: www.baem.org.uk

Cardiology

Cardiology is one of the areas of medicine in which the greatest advances have been made during the last fifteen to twenty years. As a specialty it deals with the commonest cause of death in the United Kingdom, coronary heart disease (CHD). Most efforts within the specialty have been directed at trying to deal with CHD and major advances have been made in its prevention and long-term treatment. Advances in cardiology continue and make it a very stimulating area for clinical work and research.

The consultant's job

Because cardiology is an extremely complex specialty, it provides an umbrella for many different types of physician. Some cardiologists are entirely engaged in interventional work while others are entirely engaged in preventive cardiology. Between these two extremes there are many physicians who mix different aspects of cardiology in their day-to-day working life; by far the largest group are those who work in a district general hospital (DGH). These cardiologists have to be adept in many different aspects in cardiology so that they can assess the patients who are referred to them and pass on to a tertiary centre those who require highly specialised treatment. Approximately 40 per cent of patients taken in on acute medical admission to DGHs have cardiological diseases. Cardiologists working in DGHs help run the coronary care service, assist their non-cardiological colleagues in diagnosing and treating heart disease, and run a non-invasive service with echocardiography and specialised forms of ECG monitoring. Many cardiologists are involved in the simpler forms of cardiac catheterisation and coronary angiography, with a major move over the last few years for such procedures to be carried out in the DGH. This comprehensive package of care is far more convenient for the patient and also gives the DGH cardiologist a much higher level of job satisfaction.

In the tertiary (specialist) centre the main difference is the availability of cardiac surgery. This allows complex interventional cardiology to be carried out safely with surgical cover. The cardiologists working in the tertiary centre usually provide all the services provided by the DGH but also provides extremely specialised services for patients referred from elsewhere. The more important specialised interventional services include angioplasty, valvuloplasty and electrophysiology. The care of adults with congenital heart disease is also very complicated and often requires the help of specialists from tertiary centres.

Training requirements

Trainees will start higher training in cardiology after completing general professional training, having gained MRCP (or equivalent). The duration of higher training is six years with or without dual accreditation with G(I)M. The first five years of this training will be regarded as basic training in cardiology. The final year will be subspecialty training at an advanced level; basic training in these subspecialties will occur during the first five years along with general cardiological training. Those wishing to acquire dual certification in cardiology and general medicine may do general medicine in this final year. Training includes one year of research (usually in the fourth or fifth year of training) but further research may be undertaken at the discretion of the postgraduate establishment.

Career prospects

The main trends in cardiology are towards preventive cardiology; statin drugs will certainly have a role to play here over the next few years. Another major change is the movement of investigational cardiology and cardiac catheterisation from tertiary centres to the DGH. Most DGHs in the country now have one consultant cardiologist and currently the move is for a second and even a third cardiologist to be appointed.

The ultimate aim of all cardiologists is to put themselves out of business by becoming so effective in preventing coronary artery disease that it is no longer a problem. However, this is highly unlikely to occur over the next 50 years. It is probable there will be major changes in the incidence of coronary artery disease and the patients who are treated will become progressively older as the effects of the disease are postponed by modern treatment. This in itself will produce challenges and help maintain the fascination of cardiology as a specialty.

Further information

The British Cardiac Society (BCS)
9 Fitzroy Square
London W1P 5AH
Tel: 020 7383 3887
Fax: 020 7388 0903
E-mail: enquiries@bcs.com
Website: www.bcs.org.uk

Specialist Advisory Committee for Cardiology
Royal College of Physicians
11 St Andrews Place
Regent's Park
London NW1 4LE
Tel: 020 7935 1174
Fax: 020 7486 4160
Website: www.rcplondon.ac.uk/jchmt
Secretary: Dr P Mills
Secretariat: Emma Spurgeon

Clinical genetics

Clinical genetics is a relatively new specialty, so many recently qualified doctors are unsure as to what it involves and whether it might suit them, especially as even now many undergraduate courses are inadequate or not particularly relevant. We are a small, informal and friendly specialty, so read on to see if you might be interested.

The consultant's job

You will be a clinical specialist – not a laboratory person, though you will have close links with genetics laboratories and will have had lab experience at some point in your training. You will also be interested in research, and will want to continue doing this throughout your career, though it will be clinically oriented and collaborative for most people. Most of your work will involve seeing people, often healthy relatives as well as 'patients', so you will need to be good at communicating with people. Your clinical work will involve a wide range of genetic disorders, covering all ages and fields. As 'the last generalist' you will need to have broad experience, a sharp eye in diagnosis, and an ability to know when to involve others.

Consultant posts are based in university teaching hospitals, often alongside an academic research unit and the regional genetics laboratories. The 'team' will contain other consultants, with complementary interests, as well as genetics nurse specialists and associates who form an integral part of the genetic counselling service. There is often responsibility for running peripheral clinics in your region as well as specialist clinics involving your particular area of interest. Most of a consultant's work will be outpatient based, although there will be ward referrals and may be a need to admit some patients for investigation. Add to all this, postgraduate and undergraduate teaching, laboratory liaison, audit and research, and you will be kept busy. Private practice does not figure significantly in clinical genetics.

Training requirements

People come into clinical genetics from a wide range of backgrounds, paediatrics and adult internal medicine being the commonest. A wide range of post-qualification jobs is important – plan this ahead if you know when you qualify that you want to enter Clinical Genetics. Pass your MRCP (or equivalent) before you get diverted into interesting genetics research, but often this spell in research will stand you in good stead in competing for SpR posts as would doing one of the MSc courses in Human or medical genetics.

You can find training details in the clinical genetics SAC booklet. If you do not have a genetics degree of some type, you will need to fit basic genetics into your training period, which is at present 4 years. Most of your training will involve rotating through the different areas of the Medical Genetics Service (including the laboratories) but your clinical role will rapidly become relatively independent. Your main base will be the regional medical genetics centre, but some centres have links abroad which may allow you to 'step out' for a year or more and get wider experience or a higher degree. Your regular work should provide plenty of ideas for research, if you have not already developed a particular area of research, and this will be encouraged by most consultants and your fellow trainees being involved in research.

Career prospects

Small specialties can easily swing from extreme shortage of people to being oversubscribed; in a rapidly developing field like genetics it is difficult to predict how things will develop. However our field has a good track record of 'fine-tuning' supply and demand, and there is certainly every sign that the specialty of clinical genetics will continue to be in strong demand. Recent trends have shown this especially in 'adult' areas such as cancer genetics, but dysmorphology and the field of development remains in strong demand.

Before applying for a clinical genetics training post ask around widely, visit your regional centre, talk with trainees already in the field, and attend some of the regular genetics meetings. A clinical research fellowship on a genetic topic will be of equal value in a future genetics career or back in your parent discipline.

Further information

British Society for Human Genetics
Clinical Genetics Unit, Birmingham Women's Hospital
Birmingham B15 2TG
Tel/fax: 0121 627 2634
E-mail: bshg@bshg.org.uk
Website: www.bshg.org.uk

Joint Committee on Medical Genetics (RCP, BSHG, RCPath)
Royal College of Physicians
(Chair: Professor PA Farndon, Birmingham)

Specialist Advisory Committee for Clinical Genetics
Royal College of Physicians
11 St Andrews Place
Regent's Park
London NW1 4LE
Tel: 020 7935 1174
Fax: 020 7486 4160
Website: www.rcplondon.ac.uk/jchmt

Further reading

Clinical Genetics into the 21st Century. London: Royal College of Physicians, 1996

Clinical neurophysiology

Clinical neurophysiology is a relatively new and expanding specialty in the area of diagnostic neurology which employs electrophysiological techniques to investigate the central and peripheral nervous systems. Although the last few years has seen a steady increase in consultant numbers there is a shortage of suitably trained applicants for training and consultant posts. The three main areas of the discipline include electroencephalography (EEG), evoked potentials (EP) and combined nerve conduction studies (NCS), and electromyography (EMG).

The consultant's job

Most consultants are based in regional or sub-regional neuroscience centres, while those in district general hospitals work in collaboration with neurologists and have access to nearby regional neuroscience centres. Electroencephalograms and most evoked potentials are performed by suitably trained and qualified neurophysiological technologists, but all clinical interpretation of the records and the peripheral NCS and EMG procedures are the responsibility of the consultant clinical neurophysiologist and the SpR. The consultant has overall responsibility for running and supervising the technical aspects of the department. Recent developments in per-operative monitoring and video-telemetry recordings have expanded the role of the clinical neurophysiologist and this has led to a wide spectrum of differing emphases in workloads in different departments.

Training requirements

Entry to the training programme in clinical neurophysiology requires the completion of a minimum of two years GPT in approved posts and the MRCP (UK) or (I). A period of experience in adult or paediatric neurology at SHO grade (not more than six months) is desirable. The SpR training programme is four years, based in teaching hospitals or other major centres with academic activity. It includes one year in neurology, two years in clinical neurophysiology and the balance of one year in clinical neurophysiology or approved research. Dual certification in clinical neurophysiology and neurology can be achieved if the trainee completes four years in neurology, and two years in clinical neurophysiology and one year in neurology, neurophysiology or research.

Career prospects

There is an increasing demand for fully trained clinical neuro-physiologists and the prospects for obtaining a specialist registrar training post and subsequent consultant post in either a regional neuroscience centre in a teaching hospital or neuroscience centre in a major district general hospital are excellent.

Further information

Specialist Advisory Committee for Clinical Neurophysiology
Royal College of Physicians
11 St Andrews Place
Regent's Park
London NW1 4LE
Tel: 020 7935 1174
Fax: 020 7486 4160
Website: www.rcplondon.ac.uk/jchmt

Clinical pharmacology & therapeutics

Clinical pharmacology and therapeutics (CPT) is one of the younger and smaller specialties in the UK, currently with around 70 recognised consultant posts. These posts are held mainly in academic departments associated with medicine or pharmacology, although a number are NHS funded. CPT is all about drugs as medicines, and provides an important bridge between the basic sciences and clinical medicine. A career in CPT offers the exciting prospect of a wide variety of opportunities and challenges ranging from the understanding of mechanisms of disease to the development of new drugs and the implementation of safe and rational prescribing at an individual and population level. The principal academic forum in CPT is the British Pharmacological Society, linking basic science with clinical practice and academia with the pharmaceutical industry and biotechnology.

The consultant's job

Consultant clinical pharmacologists are generally found in university posts (Senior Lecturer, Reader or Professor) and most hold honorary NHS clinical commitments, mainly but not exclusively in general (internal) medicine. There is a history of close links to cardiovascular medicine, but there are important strengths in gastroenterology, respiratory medicine and neurology, as well as the potential for links with other colleges; for instance in paediatrics, intensive care medicine and psychiatry. Most consultants will have a significant commitment to research and teaching. Many will run substantial research programmes and/or clinical trials units. Larger academic centres will look to their clinical pharmacologists to play a leading role in running drug & therapeutics committees, appraising new drugs, and to developing rational prescribing policies, treatment guidelines and drug formularies. Some consultants have developed a particular interest in toxicology and run one of the UK's network of Poisons Information Units. Many clinical pharmacologists go on to provide advice to the UK drug regulatory authorities (eg the Medicines Control Agency and Committee on Safety of Medicines).

Training requirements

The principal requirement to be a clinical pharmacologist is an active interest in the mechanisms of drug action and the discovery of new therapeutic approaches to disease. After general professional training in medicine, prospective candidates need to secure a Specialist Registrar (SpR) post. Although some will embark on a period of research before entering the SpR grade, most will undertake a higher degree (PhD or MD) during their training. Indeed, research is an embedded part of training in CPT, which is one of only a few specialties recognising two years spent in supervised research. The flexibility of the specialty, and the focus on research, allows the trainee to remain partially undifferentiated and follow research and clinical interests through organ systems; to allow a smooth transition to an academic career path. The length of training depends on whether a CCST sought in CPT alone (four years; unusual), in conjunction with one other specialty such as general (internal) medicine (five years; common) or with two other specialties (seven years; perhaps more common in future). Opportunities to train in CPT have been strengthened in recent years with the development of additional SpR training posts funded jointly by the NHS and Association of the British Pharmaceutical Industry (ABPI) in recognition of the UK need for high quality CPT.

Career prospects

A major advantage of the training in CPT is the wealth of opportunities for career development. Indeed, although the number of consultant posts in clinical pharmacology is relatively small, there is currently no prospect of unemployment for those trained in the specialty. Possible avenues, in addition to pursuing an academic or NHS career in CPT, include posts in the drug regulatory authorities or in industry. The need for an increasing focus on rational and cost effective prescribing, recognised by government and clinicians alike, should remain a key activity of CPT in the foreseeable future. The pharmaceutical industry is among the most successful of the UK's export activities, and allows opportunities to contribute to drug development and develop management and commercial skills. Here, CPT links are with the Faculty of Pharmaceutical Medicine of the Royal College of Physicians and with the ABPI. Clinical pharmacologists have always been well represented in senior positions in UK medicine – within national organisations including the Royal Colleges, the NHS and CSM – with the result that the availability of posts and prospects for promotion continue to look promising.

Further information

British Pharmacological Society
Clinical Pharmacology Section
16 Angel Gate
City Road
London EC1V 2SG
Tel: 020 7417 0113
Fax: 020 7417 0114
E-mail: sjs@bphs.org.uk
Website: www.bphs.org.uk
Honorary Clinical Secretary: Dr WW Yeo
Chairman, Clinical Pharmacology Section: Dr DN Bateman
Executive Officer: Sarah-Jane Stagg

Joint Committee on Higher Medical Training
Specialist Advisory Committee on Clinical Pharmacology and Therapeutics
5 St Andrews Place
Regent's Park
London NW1 4LB
Tel: 020 7935 1174
Fax: 020 7486 4160
Website: www.rcplondon.ac.uk/jchmt
Secretary: Professor N Benjamin
Secretariat: Kate Hope

Association of British Pharmaceutical Industry
12 Whitehall
London SW1A 2DY
Tel: 020 7930 3477
Fax: 020 7747 1413
E-mail: rtiner@abpi.org.uk
Website: www.abpi.org.uk
Contact: Dr R Tiner

Dermatology

Dermatology is a medical specialty in which clinicians also have an opportunity to develop sub-specialist skills ranging from photobiology to surgery. Insights into the pathogenesis of many skin diseases have been provided by research in fields such as skin biology, molecular genetics and immunopathology. This modern image of dermatology is largely responsible for its present popularity as a career option. Skin diseases are common and some knowledge of dermatology will help any doctor who looks after patients.

The consultant's job

Dermatologists are skilled clinicians and are less reliant on laboratory or invasive diagnostic tests than many other specialists; diagnosis still depends mainly on visual skills. Dermatology is predominantly an outpatient specialty and many consultants work in more than one hospital. Most dermatologists provide a general dermatological service (including some paediatric dermatology) in addition to one or more specialised services such as contact allergy testing, phototherapy or skin surgery. Some surgical procedures such as cryosurgery, curettage and skin biopsies may be performed during routine outpatient clinics, while other surgery may be carried out in an outpatient theatre session; many dermatologists have expertise in dermatopathology. With the increase in skin cancer many larger departments have appointed a dermatological surgeon who takes on complex cancer surgery or provides specialised services such as laser surgery. Dermatologists are also frequently asked to provide medico-legal reports because skin diseases are a common reason for disablement benefit or spells of certified incapacity to work. Most outpatients are treated in day-treatment centres but patients with severe skin problems need admission to hospital. Inpatient beds may be centralised in a dedicated dermatology unit or dedicated beds may be present on general medical wards.

Consultant dermatologists are responsible for training junior staff and teaching general practitioners. Teaching hospitals are usually staffed by one or more specialist registrars in addition to one or more SHOs; clinical assistants, associate specialists or staff grade doctors may assist the consultant in outpatient clinics.

Training requirements

Applicants for Higher Medical Training (HMT) in dermatology should have completed a minimum of two years General Professional Training (GPT) in approved posts and obtained the MRCP. Previous experience in dermatology is not essential for enrolment into HMT, but some exposure to dermatology is considered desirable, although no more than six months would be allowable towards GPT. At present the duration of HMT in dermatology is four years. The programme to which trainees are appointed will have named consultant trainers for each stage of HMT, and a period of supervised clinical or laboratory research of high quality is considered desirable. All trainees should have a non-resident on-call commitment for dermatology for the first and at least two of the three remaining years of HMT. Most training is in the outpatient department, so it is easier to train flexibly in dermatology than in many acute medical specialties. Not all DGHs have specialist registrars although most specialist registrars in dermatology will spend some time working in a DGH during their training.

Clinical and laboratory research or further special training may be taken either as a block or as protected time alongside standard clinical training from year two of HMT onwards, and trainees are encouraged, but not obliged, to submit an MD thesis based on their research. Some trainees may wish to take time out of the training programme to work towards a PhD.

Career prospects

In recent years there has been an expansion in UK dermatology consultant posts to over 350 posts. At any given time the specialty has over 100 specialist registrars in training. A small proportion will be in flexible training programmes. There is an enormous demand for dermatological care from patients. Many doctors, including those in general practice, have had limited training in dermatology and there will always be a great need for specialist dermatologists. Therefore career prospects are good. Most dermatologists become fascinated by the diversity of skin pathology and the majority of consultants are very happy with their chosen specialty.

Further information

British Association of Dermatologists
19 Fitzroy Square
London W1P 5HQ
Tel: 020 7383 0266
Fax: 020 7388 5263
Websites: www.bad.org.uk
           www.skinhealth.co.uk

Specialist Advisory Committee for Dermatology
Royal College of Physicians
11 St Andrews Place
Regent's Park
London NW1 4LE
Tel: 020 7935 1174
Fax: 020 7486 4160
Website: www.rcplondon.ac.uk/jchmt
Secretary: Dr D Roberts

Endocrinology and diabetes mellitus

Physicians with an interest in this joint specialty practice with a diverse mix of the two sub-specialities and nearly all are involved in acute general (internal) medicine. There are relatively few pure endocrinologists in the UK, mainly in teaching centres. By contrast many specialists practice in diabetes and not endocrinology, leaving this to other colleagues within their district or nearby. Increasingly the pure diabetologists also take an interest in lipid disorders, and occasionally other metabolic diseases.

The consultant's job

The mix of specialty activity with acute medicine is gradually changing with the appointment of more and more specialists in medicine, so that acute commitments are less frequent but often busier. Accordingly while a 40 per cent: 45 per cent: 15 per cent, acute: diabetes: endocrinology mix might be average, it is no longer typical due to wide variations between posts.

Diabetes care has shown speedy evolution in the last two decades, the physician role changing from the individual diagnosis-treatment doctor to the manager and member of an integrated preventive care team. Accordingly skills of management and negotiation, organisation and information technology, and education and counselling, have become more important, while technical medical skill development is centring on the broader range of drugs and insulins now reaching the market. An ability to reach into an individual patient's environment is a core skill, as well as the ability to handle multiple medical problems (mainly arterial risk factors) at one time. Apart from their own team members (specialist nurses, dieticians, podiatrists and others), specialists will need to work closely with general practitioners, ophthalmologists, vascular surgeons, cardiologists, obstetricians, and others. Some joint clinics, in particular in obstetrics, are a feature of diabetes care, as increasingly are lipid clinics.

The nature of endocrinological practice varies considerably between specialists. Many will be concerned overwhelmingly with thyroid disease, and to a smaller extent with confirming the early diagnosis of other endocrine disorders. While the diagnostic tools of endocrinology are now widely available, the number of cases of many disorders seen in an average district population is low. With more sophisticated specialist management becoming routine, expertise is often becoming concentrated in fewer hands, even in centres with more than one endocrinological specialist. Sub-specialisation is thus becoming more common.

Both specialties are now overwhelmingly outpatient based. Diabetes increasingly is located in a resource centre, while endocrinology depends on hospital clinics and ambulatory investigation units. Endocrinology research is often dependent on a good university resource base; in theory diabetes research offers good opportunities for healthcare research in any environment.

Training requirements

It is currently an assumption that specialist registrar training for dual accreditation with general (internal) medicine will average six years. This is calculated on the basis of four years of clinical work in diabetes/endocrinology and general medicine, one year in research or other health care related activity and one year on average for additional research time and finding a suitable post. For European specialty reasons certification is given in 'endocrinology', even to diabetologists with no expertise in endocrinology. Research opportunities seem good at present and most new specialists still have an MD or even PhD.

The present training structure is not flexible enough to address the needs of the individual trainee who may want to take an interest in 'non-core' areas such as lipid disorders. The curriculum is under review although some elements of the present curriculum's formal structure of minimal attendance at certain numbers of types of clinic and activities are likely to remain. However, there is a keenness to recognise that the span of training desired by each individual may legitimately show particular bias, and that the diabetes element means that an understanding of behavioural medicine and educational principles and the acquisition of managerial skills have become important.

The UK has an excellent programme of society, national, and regional educational meetings, co-ordinated through the College. Post-certification support for continuing professional development is also strong.

Career prospects

Diabetes and endocrinology is a major specialty with consultant numbers growing for the last fifteen years towards 500 in England and Wales. The

College has identified a need to double consultant numbers. Current Specialist Registrar numbers are well matched to the 4–5 per cent consultant expansion rate that has been averaged in the 1990s, but as in other specialities a small variation from this in either direction rapidly creates a mismatch between newly trained doctors and posts. The College has worked closely with specialist societies since 1984 on manpower planning in this area. Teaching hospital posts are not easy to find and, as noted above, most pure endocrinology posts are in teaching centres.

Further information

Specialty Advisory Committee for Endocrinology & Diabetes Mellitus
Royal College of Physicians
11 St Andrews Place
Regent's Park
London NW1 4LE
Tel: 020 7935 1174
Fax: 020 7486 4160
Website: www.rcplondon.ac.uk/jchmt
Secretary: Dr RW Bilous
Secretariat: Emma Spurgeon

The British Diabetic Association
10 Queen Anne Street
London W1M 0BD
Tel: 020 7323 1531
Fax: 020 7637 3644
E-mail: bda@diabetes.org.uk
Website: www.diabetes.org.uk

British Endocrine Societies
c/o Society for Endocrinology
17/18 The Courtyard
Woodlands, Bradley Stoke
Bristol BS32 4NQ
Tel: 01454 619036 (Society for Endocrinology)
            01454 619347 (BES)
Fax: 01454 616071
E-mail: info@endocrinology.org
Website: www.endocrinology.org

Gastroenterology

Gastroenterology is one of the most technical of the medical specialties but also encompasses a wide range of clinical problems, including benign and malignant diseases of the upper and lower intestine, acute and chronic liver disease and pancreatic disease. It also includes some of the greatest challenges for clinical research such as inflammatory bowel disease, hepatitis, liver failure, functional bowel syndromes, gastrointestinal bleeding and several of the commonest cancers.

The consultant's job

Most gastroenterologists maintain a commitment to involvement in acute internal medicine but outpatient referrals are predominantly gastroenterological. It is increasingly common for hospitals to have at least two consultants in the specialty. The increasing complexity of investigational and therapeutic techniques has led increasingly to subspecialisation, often with one consultant, or group of consultants, having a particular expertise in hepatobiliary disease and the other having expertise in luminal gastroenterology, including inflammatory bowel disease. Liver transplantation is focussed at supra-regional centres and cases with severe acute liver failure are increasingly based at these centres because of the use of liver transplantation as part of its management. Work practices vary according to the size of hospital and degree of subspecialisation but a consultant will commonly have two outpatient sessions and two or three endoscopy sessions per week; additional sessions might include a subspecialty interest such as nutrition, motility or endoscopic ultrasound. Gastroenterologists work closely with gastrointestinal surgeons in providing care for patients with inflammatory bowel disease, gastrointestinal cancer and pancreato-biliary disease. There is also close collaboration with diagnostic and interventional radiology and histopathology and in most centres regular weekly clinical meetings will occur jointly with these specialties.

Training requirements

Specialist training in gastroenterology and general internal medicine is given during a five-year specialist registrar rotation following successful completion of the MRCP diploma. This should usually include training up to a good degree of proficiency in diagnostic and therapeutic upper and lower intestinal endoscopy. It is becoming increasingly difficult for a trainee to become fully proficient in all possible aspects of interventional gastroenterology such as therapeutic biliary endoscopy and endoscopic ultrasound within the specialist registrar period. It is likely to be increasingly accepted that consultants will offer proficiency in a range of appropriate procedures rather than providing comprehensive expertise.

Although the need for all trainees to do research as a prerequisite for career advancement is less certain than in the past, there is a clear need for gastroenterological research to be continued by clinicians. Many of the important clinical problems such as inflammatory bowel disease, acute liver failure, functional bowel disease, gastro-intestinal bleeding are not going to be solved by basic scientists working in isolation and this is one of the attractions of gastroenterology as a clinical specialty. Research can be undertaken at any point in the training but it is more practical to start research either shortly after obtaining MRCP or in the earlier years of the specialist registrar rotation. Substantial research leading to an MD or PhD will usually require two to three years separately funded outside of the specialist registrar rotation although some training accreditation may be allowed for this if it occurs after the award of a national training number.

Career prospects

Prospects are currently good. An accurate manpower database is continually updated and the numbers of trainees and potential consultant posts look to be in balance. The pressure of diagnostic and therapeutic waiting lists is continuing to drive an expansion in consultant numbers but much depends on the rate of expansion being continued or accelerated over the next ten years.

Further information

British Society of Gastroenterology
3 St Andrews Place
Regent's Park
London NW1 4LB
Tel: 020 7387 3534
            020 7935 2815
Fax: 020 7487 3734
E-mail: bsg@mailbox.ulcc.ac.uk
Website: www.bsg.org.uk

Trainees in Gastroenterology (TIGS)
c/o Diane Mathias
Administrative Secretary
7 Trehern Road
London SW14 8PD
Tel: 020 8876 6317

Specialist Advisory Committee for Gastroenterology
Royal College of Physicians
11 St Andrews Place
Regent's Park
London NW1 4LE
Tel: 020 7935 1174
Fax: 020 7486 4160
Website: www.rcplondon.ac.uk/jchmt
Secretary: Dr RP Walt
Secretariat: Kate Hope

General internal medicine

General medicine is the backbone of internal medicine and integral to all parts of medicine. The founding fathers of the Royal College in 1518 were true general physicians, handling all varieties of medical problems. Over the centuries areas of medicine have budded off as separate specialties, fuelled by advances in science and knowledge. This has accelerated in the last two decades with more and more pressure to specialise; as a result tensions have developed between the generalist and the specialist. Patients and GPs want the best possible specialist to look at specific problems but the generalist is still required when the diagnosis is uncertain or there is multi-system disease. Despite the pressures, general medicine is still the largest specialty in medicine with most people accrediting and training in both general medicine and a specialty. It is also worth stressing that to be a good specialist requires knowledge of medicine outside one's own specialty.

The consultant's job

General internal medicine (GIM) comprises four components: acute unselected medicine (the first twenty-four hours); continuing care of the acutely admitted patient; unselected general medicine outpatient clinics; and any specialty that is not your own. You may be appointed either as a general physician with an interest in a specialty, or – more likely these days – a specialist undertaking general medical duties. In either case, you will be expected to cover general medical admissions on anything from a 1-in-5 to a 1-in-10 basis, depending on the numbers of physicians sharing the on-call rota. You may be supported by a specialist registrar, but at least a quarter of you will have only senior house officer and house officer support. Typically you will admit from fifteen to fifty patients and may have twelve hour split shifts. Most people will have an admissions ward and will hand over patients to appropriate specialists the next day, although you will tend to retain about half the admitted patients. There may be an age-related admissions policy, although more and more geriatricians play a full, integrated role in emergency admissions.

An admitting general physician will always do a post-take ward round, as recommended by the College. You will probably have a follow-up clinic for patients following acute admissions. It is possible that you will also see unselected new referrals in this clinic, but in many places the numbers so referred are diminishing and one of your colleagues may see all such patients.

Training requirements

Trainees in GIM will always have undertaken a minimum two years general professional training (GPT) in approved SHO posts and have passed the MRCP. Many will often have spent an additional year as a 'senior' SHO – excellent experience. Trainees are then able to enrol for higher medical training as an SpR, with the ultimate aim to receive the certificate of completion of specialist training (CCST) and be admitted onto the specialist register. All trainees are advised to undertake GIM training as well as a specialty, although at consultant level you are most likely to do general acute medicine if your specialty is cardiology, endocrinology and diabetes, gastroenterology, geriatrics or thoracic medicine; a significant number of nephrologists and rheumatologists also do acute medicine. Such dual accreditation training programmes last five or six years. Full details of the required training programmes can be found in the JCHMT handbook. There is considerable flexibility in the way GIM is integrated with specialty training, but experience of acute medicine should be obtained in the last two years as well as earlier. There are however likely to be significant changes in the way training is organised in GIM in the near future.

Career prospects

There is no shortage of work or jobs in GIM – the problems arise in the associated specialty. There is considerable satisfaction to be gained in working as a general physician. It is challenging, but can be frustrating if the workload is too heavy. Before applying for a post it is worth establishing clearly how emergency admissions are organised, what support is available, how often you will be on take and whether there is an admissions ward and good nursing support.

Further information

General (Internal) Medicine Committee
Royal College of Physicians
11 St Andrews Place
Regent's Park
London NW1 4LE
Tel: 020 7935 1174
Fax: 020 7487 5218
Website: www.rcplondon.ac.uk

Consultant physicians working for patients. Part 1: a blue-print for effective hospital practice. Part 2: job plans for specialist physicians. London: RCP, 1999.

Rhodes JM, Harrison B, Black D, Spiro S, *et al.* General internal medicine and specialty medicine – time to rethink the relationship. *J R Coll Physicians Lond* 1999; 33: 341–7.

Joint Committee on Higher Medical Training (JCHMT)
5 St Andrews Place
Regent's Park
London NW1 4LB
Tel: 020 7935 1174
Fax: 020 7486 4160
E-mail: jchmt@rcplondon.ac.uk

JCHMT Training Handbook *(annual revision)*

Specialist Advisory Committee for General Internal Medicine
Royal College of Physicians
11 St Andrews Place
Regent's Park
London NW1 4LE
Tel: 020 7935 1174
Fax: 020 7486 4160
Website: www.rcplondon.ac.uk/jchmt
Secretary: Dr C Mitchell
Secretariat: Kate Forrester

Genitourinary medicine

The increasing varieties of sexually transmitted organisms recognised in recent years and the currently rising incidence of most sexually transmitted infections (STIs) combine to offer the prospect of a fascinating and stimulating career. In the UK specialists in genitourinary (GU) medicine tend to practise exclusively in this discipline. GU medicine clinics provide ready access for patients whose prompt management plays a major role in minimising the incidence of all STIs, including human immunodeficiency virus (HIV) infection, in the UK.

The consultant's job

GU medicine consultants undertake most of their clinical work in outpatient departments, usually in dedicated premises, with support from specialist nurses and other staff. For many STIs clinical examination is supported by laboratory tests, some performed within the clinic for quick confirmation of clinical diagnoses. A wide variety of problems are seen ranging from acute conditions responding quickly to a short course of an antimicrobial, to chronic viral and other conditions which are difficult and challenging to manage. The latter includes HIV infection; most of the outpatient and day care of patients with HIV infection is provided in GU clinics while many consultants also take all or a share of the responsibility for their inpatient care. The specialty now encompasses many subspecialty interests in addition to the care of STIs and HIV infection, including colposcopy, the care of vulval disease, psychosexual problems including the management of male impotence, and care of rape victims, while most clinics provide family planning services.

Training requirements

The Higher Medical Training programme for GU medicine requires applicants to have completed a minimum of two years of GPT and to have obtained the MRCP. An alternative is the MRCOG. A trainee with the MRCP requires gynaecology training during their GPT, preferably as a six-month post in gynaecology or obstetrics & gynaecology. MRCOG holders currently must spend at least one year after registration in posts approved for GPT in general internal medicine, including on-call for emergencies.

The four-year training programme is divided into two stages. Years one and two provide a sound, broad, general knowledge of STIs including HIV infection, and family planning, education, prevention, contact tracing to limit spread of infection, and screening to prevent cervical cancer. Trainees learn research methods (including statistics) and initiate research projects. A maximum of one year devoted to research can be counted towards training, preferably directed towards an MD or PhD. Trainees will become proficient at the laboratory procedures undertaken in the clinic and spend sufficient time in laboratories to learn to interpret reports. In years three and four these basic skills are consolidated. In addition, special skills are developed such as colposcopy and HIV care including inpatient management. An on-call commitment is provided to ensure experience in managing acute problems. Trainees learn management skills, audit and teaching skills. Overseas experience can be included but needs approval in advance by the SAC in GU medicine.

Career prospects

GU clinics are mainly situated in general hospitals, and all cities and most towns have a clinic; large cities have several clinics. This offers the possibility of a wide variety of posts. Major university hospitals have teams of consultants working in an academic environment of teaching and research and may see many HIV affected patients; consultants have an opportunity to pursue a subspecialty while contributing to general patient care. At the other end of a spectrum are smaller clinics in market towns where consultants single-handedly concentrate on treating non-HIV sexually transmitted diseases.

The number of consultant posts has almost doubled in the last decade though expansion is currently slower. Consultants in GU medicine have always enjoyed more mobility than those in other specialties. Currently numbers of training posts are being slightly increased indicating that in future there will be ample opportunity for energetic, hard-working doctors to make a career in this specialty.

Further information

Secretariat, Medical Society for the Study of Venereal Diseases,
Royal Society of Medicine,
1 Wimpole Street
London W1M 8AE
Tel: 020 7290 2968/3904
Fax: 020 7290 2989
E-mail: Enquiries@mssvd.org.uk
Website: www.mssvd.org.uk

Association for Genito-Urinary Medicine
c/o Department of GU Medicine
Newcastle General Hospital
Westgate Road
Newcastle-upon-Tyne NE4 6BE
Website: www.agum.org.uk
Chair: Dr JRW Harris

Specialist Advisory Committee for Genitourinary Medicine
Royal College of Physicians
11 St Andrews Place
Regent's Park
London NW1 4LE
Tel: 020 7935 1174
Fax: 020 7486 4160
Website: www.rcplondon.ac.uk/jchmt
Secretary: Dr J Wilson
Secretariat: Cath Janion

Geriatric medicine

An enthusiastic but realistic approach to the investigation and management of older people presenting with a variety of symptoms is the *raison d'être* of geriatrics, which is still a truly general specialty. It is therefore an attractive proposition for doctors who enjoy general medicine and working as part of a team, who also have a high level of clinical and leadership skills. Increasingly consultant posts are integrated, and practise both acute general medicine and geriatric medicine, but some posts will remain in geriatric medicine alone. There are many opportunities for innovation and development, both personal and professional, within the specialty.

The consultant's job

Besides acute general medical care, the rehabilitation of older people lies at the core of the geriatrician's job as a leading member of the multi-disciplinary team. There is some involvement in aspects of long-term care and in close working with GPs, social services and voluntary agencies. There are many exciting opportunities to plan and develop new services both in hospitals and the community. Geriatric medicine covers a wide range of facilities sometimes on multiple sites, which combine local accessibility with central specialist services. Most geriatricians also have a sub-specialty interest, which can be developed as part of the overall service. Junior staff training is an important part of the consultant's work and geriatric medicine offers a wide variety of experience to junior staff in many disciplines.

Training requirements

A wide experience in general medicine is required, and posts in related fields such as general practice, neurology and psychiatry are particularly useful. MRCP or equivalent is essential, and some time spent working in a geriatric department is recommended before committing oneself to the specialty. Most training schemes now provide dual accreditation in general medicine and geriatric medicine over five years, thus offering the widest choice of consultant posts, but there are some programmes available to those who wish to obtain accreditation in geriatric medicine alone. All specialist registrar training programmes in the UK have a requirement to develop experience in research: this may be by undertaking a course in research methodologies, by having a defined research post for up to one year of the training rotation, or by being involved with an ongoing research project over the period of training. Trainees are encouraged to publish their projects and to present papers at regional and national meetings to enable them to continue to develop throughout their consultant career. For those with particular aptitude and interest in research, there are good opportunities for academic posts in geriatric medicine and gerontology.

Career prospects

Career prospects in geriatric medicine are good, particularly for those who undertake dual accreditation in general medicine and geriatrics. There are increasing opportunities for part time work and job sharing, which makes the specialty particularly attractive to those with domestic commitments who wish to retain and develop an interesting and rewarding career.

Further information

British Geriatric Society
1 St Andrews Place
Regent's Park
London NW1 4LB
Tel: 020 79354004
Fax: 020 72240454
E-mail: info@bgs.org.uk
Website: www.bgs.org.uk

British Geriatric Society (BGS) National Training Committee, regional advisers, regional training chairmen, and regional academic leads can all be contacted through the BGS as above.

Specialist Advisory Committee for Geriatric Medicine
Royal College of Physicians
11 St Andrews Place
Regent's Park
London NW1 4LE
Tel: 020 7935 1174
Fax: 020 7486 4160
Website: www.rcplondon.ac.uk/jchmt
Secretary: Dr T Hendra
Secretariat: Kate Forrester

Haematology

Haematology was the first specialty to bring together training in both the laboratory and clinical aspects of the subject. This has produced a splendidly varied discipline in which the management of patients and their diseases is based firmly on direct understanding of the pathology.

The consultant's job

Consultant haematologists will see and manage patients of all ages with a wide variety of clinical problems, benign as well as malignant. Modern, intensive treatment of malignant diseases such as the leukaemias and lymphomas mean that haematologists have to have expertise in acute medicine, including aspects of intensive care and in the delivery of high dose chemotherapy. The consultant will need to manage and advise on problems of thrombosis and haemostasis, often being involved with other disciplines; he/she will also need to have the skills to investigate and treat the many causes of anaemia both acquired and inherited. Part of the pleasure of being a consultant haematologist comes from the opportunities to collaborate with colleagues in other fields in the control of disorders of the blood. Much of this collaboration starts with the laboratory duties of the consultant, who is not only expected to examine blood films and bone marrow samples by microscopy, but is also responsible for laboratory management including coagulation and blood transfusion. Within this broad range of subjects there is the opportunity to develop individual expertise within both the clinical and laboratory aspects.

Developing and expanding aspects of haematology include transfusion medicine and the use of blood stem cell transplants in the management of the widening group of illnesses. The consultant is also responsible for overseeing the quality of the laboratory practice through the national external quality assurance schemes and will be expected to extend the quality assurance to the clinical part of the specialty, in part through clinical audit.

Training requirements

Entry to the specialty requires a basic training in medicine, ie MRCP or its equivalent. The broader the general professional training the better, with time spent in respiratory medicine, infectious diseases, clinical haematology, or oncology being especially valuable. Acquisition of technical skills with invasive procedure is also helpful. Once the candidate enters the specialist registrar grade, training in laboratory aspects of haematology should begin, including morphology, blood transfusion, haemostasis and thrombosis, and special areas such as haemoglobinopathies, haemophilia and the molecular pathology of blood diseases. This training runs parallel with training in clinical presentations of haematological disorders. Formal appraisal takes place throughout training, a two-way process with trainers and trainees. The major summative examination, MRCPath Part I, is taken after two to three years training and includes assessment of laboratory skills. The normal training period is five years and the latter part (two to three years) gives an opportunity to study in great depth certain parts of the curriculum of special interest to the individual. The majority of trainees take time out of programmes to pursue a full-time research experience at some stage during the training. At the end of training, and in order to receive the certificate of completion of specialist training (CCST) and be admitted to the Specialist Register, the trainee takes the Part II of the MRCPath which consists solely of a structured viva on a single day.

Career prospects

Haematology has always been a popular specialty, mainly because of the combination of laboratory and clinical work. About 50 % of entrants are female and the specialty is well adapted to flexible training. The ratio of trainees to consultant posts is slightly too large but continuing consultant expansion, particularly to meet the needs of improved management of haematological malignancies, has meant that there have been good prospects of acquiring a consultant post within a specified time.

Further information

British Society for Haematology
2 Carlton House Terrace
London SW1Y 5AF
Website: http://www.blacksci.co.uk/uk/society/bsh/

Royal Society of Pathologists
2 Carlton House Terrace
London SW1Y 5AF
E-mail: info@rcpath.org
Website: http://www.rcpath.org

Specialist Advisory Committee for Haematology
Royal College of Physicians
11 St Andrews Place
Regent's Park
London NW1 4LE
Tel: 020 7935 1174
Fax: 020 7486 4160
Website: www.rcplondon.ac.uk/jchmt
Secretary: Dr P Chipping
Secretariat: Cath Janion

Immunology

Immunology comprises the diagnosis and management of diseases caused directly as a result of under, over or inappropriate function of the immune system. Most of these diseases are chronic and range in severity from relatively mild conditions through to life-threatening multi-system diseases such as necrotising vasculitic disease or severe forms of immunodeficiency. Many of the more common immunological diseases are focussed on a single organ and in these examples the majority of cases are managed by the relevant clinical specialty such as rheumatology, nephrology or dermatology, often with support from immunologists in diagnosis or management. Immunologists will often take responsibility for the rarer forms of auto-immune or immunodeficiency diseases which are multi-system and require specialist evaluation and treatment. Allergy represents one of the commoner forms of immune disease resulting from inappropriate immune responses and immunologists will liaise with allergists or organ-based specialists on the diagnosis and management of the more complex forms of allergic disease.

The consultant's job

Most consultants are located in medical teaching centres or district general hospitals serving large population areas, reflecting the relatively low prevalence of many of the diseases involved. Most immunologists work in centralised facilities, usually with more than one consultant, providing a range of services.

A central responsibility is supervision of a diagnostic immunology laboratory that provides a range of investigations for the identification and management of auto-immune, immunodeficiency and allergic diseases. This role involves close oversight of results and day-to-day liaison with organ-based specialists and, increasingly, general practitioners with regard to the appropriate investigation of suspected immunological diseases.

Clinical work is largely outpatient-based and will usually involve the direct long-term management of rare primary immunodeficiency disorders and the assessment and follow-up of autoimmune or allergic disease in joint clinics with paediatricians, allergists or organ-based specialists. Other demands will depend on local circumstances and in some centres immunologists have a major input into organ transplantation programmes.

Training requirements

A Joint Committee of the Royal Colleges of Physicians and Pathologists has drawn up a training programme that reflects the requirements for both clinical and laboratory training. All entrants to the training programme will have completed general professional training at senior house officer level and have been successful in the MRCP (UK) or equivalent qualification.

The training programme is structured into an initial two-year module in which experience in clinical and laboratory immunology is underpinned by tuition in the basic science of immunology, often undertaken as an MSc course. Training at the host centre will include rotation or attachment to clinical departments dealing with immunological disease such as rheumatology, dermatology or infectious diseases, as well as secondment to national centres, for example paediatric immunology departments offering bone marrow transplantation for primary immunodeficiency diseases.

Local training is also supplemented by a two-year programme of national training days held at a number of regional centres, where specialty trainees have the opportunity to meet and interact. At the end of this two-year period, Part 1 of the membership of the Royal College of Pathologists will be taken, comprising written papers examining basic science and clinical practice of immunology, together with a practical examination and viva. Following successful completion of this examination, there is a further three years in clinical and laboratory work. In the course of this second phase of training, candidates are eligible to complete the MRCPath. examination by submission of a thesis, collection of published papers or a book of case studies, together with a clinical viva.

Most trainees will wish to undertake a period of significant research leading to an MD or PhD. A break between the first and second periods of training provides a suitable opportunity to undertake this if appropriate grant support can be obtained. Those considering entry into immunology as a career are strongly advised to obtain advice by discussion with one or more consultants responsible for providing a regional immunology service.

Career prospects

Career prospects in immunology are good and most trainees will rapidly gain a consultant appointment in a teaching centre on completion of specialist training. New positions in immunology are being created as many single-handed centres are developing into teams with broader experience. The introduction of a new generation of drugs with selective actions on immunological mechanisms is likely to further increase the need for specialist immunological input into the appropriate therapy and the monitoring of treatment of chronic immunological disorders.

Further information

Specialist Advisory Committee for Immunology
Royal College of Physicians
11 St Andrews Place
Regent's Park
London NW1 4LE
Tel: 020 7935 1174
Fax: 020 7486 4160
Website: www.rcplondon.ac.uk/jchmt
Secretary: Dr A Farrell
Secretariat: Emma Spurgeon

Infectious diseases and tropical medicine

Infectious diseases have a high public profile and their prevention and management continue to consume a large portion of the health budget. New diseases and multi-resistant pathogens are constantly emerging and the roles of the different infection-related consultants are also evolving.

The consultant's job

Most consultants work in regional units that are usually based within large teaching hospitals. The major part of the workload is the diagnosis and care of patients with community-acquired infections. For many physicians this is the most satisfying part of the job, patients are often young with eminently treatable conditions that do not require long-term follow-up. These range from common problems such as gastroenteritis and hepatitis to exotic diseases such as malaria and other imported infections. Pathogens such as multi-resistant tuberculosis pose special problems both for therapy, and for the isolation of patients from the general community. Interesting and obscure presentations of non-communicable diseases are frequently encountered and infectious disease physicians must maintain their expertise in general internal medicine.

Most will be involved with the care of patients with HIV infection and its complications. This requires the ability to work with multiple agencies, and care is usually shared with colleagues from other disciplines, especially genitourinary medicine. Other infections that cross medical specialty backgrounds are tuberculosis and chronic viral hepatitis.

Within the hospital setting, the infectious disease physician plays an important part in the wider infection team, working with clinical microbiologists and virologists, infection control personnel, clinical immunologists, pharmacists and public health specialists. This includes giving advice on the management of bacteraemic patients and those with nosocomial infection in general, as well as consulting on the management of infections in hospital areas with immunocompromised patients. The continued emergence of micro-organisms that are resistant to multiple anti-microbials means that antibiotic policies need constant re-examination. Regional expertise is provided in the management of imported infections and most units run clinics to give advice to travellers.

Most consultants work in centres with at least one other infectious disease colleague. The majority also provides general internal medicine cover. A few infection specialists have sessions in public health medicine or other specialities. The ID unit is a popular clinical placement for medical students and postgraduates, and specialists usually have a heavy teaching commitment. Over half the consultant posts in England are academic appointments, with many opportunities for research.

Training requirements

Entry to Higher Medical Training must be preceded by General Professional Training and acquisition of the MRCP (UK) or equivalent. It is usual to seek dual certification in both infectious disease and general internal medicine

The increasing overlap in the consultative roles of clinical ID specialists and clinical microbiologists led to recommendations on the training for both groups being formulated by a Joint Committee of the Royal College of Physicians and of Pathologists in 1990. This called for a greater degree of exposure to each other's disciplines as part of training. In addition the two Colleges have successfully recommended the establishment of a training pathway for trainees to achieve dual accreditation in both infectious diseases and microbiology.

Detailed training programmes should be obtained from the JCHMT. At its simplest, the four year infectious disease pathway contains a mandatory core period of at least twelve months in a centre providing all-round experience of community acquired infection, and six months of clinical microbiology. Time in intensive care and in the management of patients with HIV is also essential. Additional options include prospectively approved training in the tropics for up to six months and experience in related disciplines, eg public health medicine or GUM. Up to one year may be spent in an approved centre overseas. The SAC allows for a year of time spent in research to count towards the four years and, in practice, the majority of trainees will take two to three extra years out of programme to pursue studies for a PhD or MD.

Tropical medicine is considered to be an 'extra' ID speciality, and those who wish to acquire a Tropical Medicine CCST must augment their training by pursuing an approved full-time course leading to acquisition of the Diploma in Tropical Medicine and Hygiene (or equivalent). Almost all those pursuing tropical medicine are likely to undertake substantive research overseas as part of their training. There is no pathway for training in travel medicine although a variety of diplomas and masters courses are available.

Career prospects

Despite considerable expansion over the past 15 years, there are still very few infectious disease specialists in the UK compared to our counterparts in Europe, Australasia and North America. Further NHS and academic posts may be achieved by appointment of general medicine consultants with an interest in infectious diseases in district general hospitals. We hope that the new joint training pathway will produce pluripotential specialists in infection that are attractive to NHS trusts. Almost all tropical medicine appointments at senior level are academic.

Further information

Specialist Advisory Committee for Infectious Diseases and Tropical Medicine
Royal College of Physicians
11 St Andrews Place
Regent's Park
London NW1 4LE
Tel: 020 7935 1174
Fax: 020 7486 4160
Website: www.rcplondon.ac.uk/jchmt
Secretary: Dr D Nathwani
Secretariat: Emma Spurgeon

Intensive care medicine

The Specialist Training Authority has recently granted approval for intensive care medicine (ICM) to become a specialty for the award of CCST. In the UK, ICM has traditionally been dominated by individuals trained in anaesthesia and the Intensive Care Society has currently around 1000 members, over 900 of whom cite anaesthesia as their base specialty. This phenomenon is explained partly by the requirement for all anaesthetists to gain exposure to intensive care as part of their basic and advanced training. The Intercollegiate Board for Training in ICM (based at the Royal College of Anaesthetists) is tasked with forming training programmes for individuals from a variety of base specialties, including medicine.

The consultant's job

The nature of the consultant's job in ICM depends largely upon the size and scope of the institution within which the individual intensive care unit (ICU) is located. For example, in large teaching hospitals there may be specialised, post-surgical units dealing with cardiothoracic or neurosurgical patients and high dependency units dealing with patients suffering from acute medical conditions. The separation of critical care is less likely to be encountered in smaller hospitals in which coronary care, HDU and ICU patients may be accommodated in adjoining or even common facilities. The scope and extent of the consultant's workload will also depend in part upon his or her base specialty and clinical experience. In smaller ICUs most appointments are part-time and many intensive care physicians maintain a sessional commitment both to ICU and to their base discipline (commonly respiratory medicine). By contrast, the largest ICUs are increasingly appointing substantially full-time consultant staff who frequently work in a week-on, week-off fashion, with several consultant-based ward rounds per day. The 'hands on' nature of the job dictates that consultant staff are frequently based within the ICU out of hours and at weekends. Large units are increasingly aware of the need for 'follow-up' outpatient clinics with detailed documentation and evaluation of outcome statistics.

Training requirements

Mastering a wide range of practical procedures including the insertion of intra-arterial and intravenous catheters and the airway skills necessitates advanced training in recognised training units. At present, three levels of training are emerging in ICM in the UK. It is suggested by the Royal Colleges that all individuals at SHO level planing on entering an acute care specialty should perform a minimum of three months training in ICM during their period of General Professional Training. Eventually, five year training programmes leading to a CCST in general (internal) medicine/ICM or anaesthesia are likely to emerge. However, individuals with national training numbers may already apply to enter intermediate (one year) or advanced (two year) level programmes. Individuals with a 'physicianly' background without prior experience of anaesthetics are required to carry out six months of anaesthesia in addition to six months further training in ICM before intermediate recognition can be awarded. Individuals wishing to pursue a more or less full time career in ICM are advised to undertake an advanced level, two-year programme, some six to eight of which are currently recognised around the UK. Regional educational advisers in ICM have recently been appointed with a view to supervising such posts and expanding their numbers. Recognition of training gained abroad depends upon the nature of the programmes involved, however, physicians wishing to train abroad are advised to consult the Board prior to commencing any overseas programme.

Career prospects

Intensive care facilities are under increasing pressure within the NHS and this is recognised by the recent instigation of an Audit Commission report. This, together with the emergence of the concept of the acute care physician and the recommendation that all SHOs should experience ICM, will undoubtedly lead to an expansion in the consultant grade. At present, district general hospitals frequently advertise for individuals with expertise in anaesthesia and intensive care medicine, but a number of posts have recently been advertised for individuals co-practising ICM with a medical sub-specialty. However, until demand for ICM clinicians can be determined and funding for training posts identified, these positions are unlikely to emerge in any number.

Further information

The Intensive Care Society
Tavistock House, Tavistock Square
London WC1 9HR
Tel: 020 7383 2184
Fax: 020 7388 3759
E-mail: ics@icnarc.demon.co.uk
Website: www.ncl.ac.uk/nsa/icsuk

Intercollegiate Board for Training in Intensive Care Medicine
Royal College of Anaesthetists
48–49 Russell Square
London WC1B 4JY
Tel: 020 7813 1900
Fax: 020 7813 1876
E-mail: info@rcoa.ac.uk.
Website: www.ics.ac.uk

Medical oncology

Medical oncology is a rapidly expanding specialty providing expertise in the development and delivery of drug treatments for cancer. Cancer care requires a team approach with input from oncological surgeons, clinical oncologists with expertise in radiotherapy as well as in some drug treatments, tumour pathologists, radiologists and specialist nurses. Cancer care is developing rapidly with many clinical, technical and organisational developments. Medical oncology has primarily been responsible for initiating and co-ordinating much of the clinical research in oncology and has a strong academic base.

The consultant's job

There are several different types of medical oncology consultant ranging from a district general hospital (DGH) based cancer specialist providing clinical expertise at cancer unit level across a broad range of cancers (10 per cent), through site specialised clinicians based at the cancer centre dealing with two or three different types (70 per cent), to super-specialised clinical scientists with involvement in laboratory based cancer research (20 per cent). The entire range of cancers may be seen by a medical oncologist with only a few exceptions: leukaemias are usually treated by haematologists rather than medical oncologists and paediatric tumours by specialist oncologists with specific training in paediatrics.

Medical oncologists work very closely with their radiotherapy colleagues and in many areas of cancer care there is considerable overlap in their functions and expertise. However, in most oncology centres the medical oncologists are responsible for the intensive chemotherapy treatments, sometimes including high dose chemotherapy requiring haematopoietic stem cell support, while the clinical oncologists provide all radiotherapy services and a limited range of drug treatments.

More than one half of the medical oncologists in the country have academic, university-based appointments. These posts enable collaboration with basic cancer research and the co-ordination of clinical trials. NHS based consultants will usually have outpatient clinical responsibilities at one or more of the cancer units attached to their inpatient base at the cancer centre. More recently NHS consultants have been appointed to work primarily at a cancer unit with inpatient as well as outpatient facilities at the DGH, but they will usually also spend a day a week at their regional cancer centre to facilitate specialist development, research and continuing medical education (CME).

Training requirements

Appointment to a medical oncology SpR post requires at least two years experience in general professional training and possession of the MRCP (UK). Specialist training requires a minimum of four years clinical training. In the first two years, a common core curriculum with clinical oncology trainees is taught on a day release basis at various large centres around the country. This generally leads to an MSc in Cancer Studies. Thereafter, specialist clinical training with appropriate site specialisation occurs. Currently, unlike clinical oncology, there is no exit examination.

Many medical oncology trainees take time out for research to obtain an MD or PhD. A research degree is not a mandatory training requirement, but is strongly encouraged, and there are many clinical research fellowships available for appropriate laboratory or clinical projects. Alternatively, a research fellowship may be taken up after completing general medical training but before you enter an SpR programme. This will help considerably in the competition for SpR posts, but has the disadvantage that research may not tie in with subsequent clinical interests.

Career prospects

In recent years, as a result of the rapid expansion in non-surgical oncology to enable the Calman-Hine model of cancer care to be delivered, the career prospects in medical oncology have become excellent. You need to give some thought to the type of medical oncology consultant post you would want, as this will affect some aspects of your training and the relative importance of a higher degree.

Further information

Association of Cancer Physicians (Chairman Professor TA Lister)
Department of Medicine
Royal Marsden NHS Trust
Downs Road
Sutton
Surrey SM2 5PT
Tel: 020 8661 3276
Fax: 020 8643 0373
E-mail: acp@icr.ac.uk
Central Secretariat: Ms A Norton

Medical Oncology Committee
Chair: Dr Michael Cullen, Birmingham

Specialist Advisory Committee for Medical Oncology
Royal College of Physicians
11 St Andrews Place
Regent's Park
London NW1 4LE
Tel: 020 7935 1174
Fax: 020 7486 4160
Website: www.rcplondon.ac.uk/jchmt
Secretary: Dr P Cameron

Neurology

Neurology is a growing specialty that is becoming increasingly popular although entry to the training grade has been particularly difficult since the introduction of the SpR training.

The consultant's job

No consultant neurologist should now be working in isolation and most are now linked contractually to a neurology centre. There are about 36 combined neurology and neurosurgery centres and 25 neurology centres in the UK. Many neurologists will have an arrangement to do outpatients clinics at other district general hospitals or in some areas, they may be employed and live in the district and attend the centre.

Neurology appeals to people who enjoy bedside medicine and patient contact. It requires a logical and deductive approach and is both intellectual and pragmatic. Most patients never require admission to hospital, and many never require any investigations. Basic clinical skills remain essential despite impressive advances in technological support and scientific understanding of the subject. The traditional emphasis on diagnosis remains paramount, but the modern neurologist also requires excellent communication and counselling skills and has to be prepared to take on a patient through the whole course of an illness. The neurologist often works closely with other specialists such as neurophysiologists, neuroradiologists and neurosurgeons but also with geneticists, rehabilitation specialists and many other medical specialists as well as physio- and other therapists. Neurologists are likely to become increasingly involved in the management of stroke and other neurological emergencies and possibly in non-surgical head trauma.

Training requirements

Most doctors entering the SpR grade will already have done one or more SHO posts in Neurology and some will have done some research.

Training is now organised to follow a curriculum with progression over a five-year clinical course from general neurology to specialist areas such as movement disorders, epilepsy, stroke or demyelinating disease. It is likely that research during the training years, which can give up to one year's credit against the five year course, will offer an opportunity for the doctor to study a particular area of interest over one to three years, often leading to a higher degree and a life-long interest in that area. Rotas are in general not arduous, and protected time for research and study, as well as a programme of monthly training days are a mandatory component of the years in training.

Career prospects

There is a considerable bottleneck at the stage of entry into the grade, and confusion about who was entitled to a training number in December 1996 led to large numbers of research doctors gaining the right to training. This 'bulge' has not yet been absorbed, and even when it is, there will then be five years or so of excessive numbers completing their training and having difficulties obtaining posts, which could then result in reductions of the pool of training numbers available to neurology. Those dedicated to this career are at present queuing up in LAT posts or doing research posts which give no guarantee of progression to a career post. There will always be a need for neurologists and the number of consultants is likely to grow but it would take unsustainable growth to ease the congestion on the SHO grade. Aspirant neurologists with an interest in the physiology of the nervous system should certainly consider a career in neurophysiology, and those who enjoy the management of neurological disability should consider training in rehabilitation medicine. Dual accreditation schemes are available and should become more flexible in the near future.

Further information

Association of British Neurologists
Ormond House, 4th Floor
27 Boswell Street
London WC1N 3JZ
Tel: 020 7405 4060
Fax: 020 7405 4070
E-mail: abn@abnoffice.demon.co.uk

Specialist Advisory Committee for Neurology
Royal College of Physicians
11 St Andrews Place
Regent's Park
London NW1 4LE
Tel: 020 7935 1174
Fax: 020 7486 4160
Website: www.rcplondon.ac.uk/jchmt
Secretary: Professor M Brown

Nuclear medicine

Nuclear medicine is a branch of clinical medicine, the distinctive feature of which is the use of unsealed radioactive materials for diagnosis, treatment, or research. Nuclear medicine procedures are now widely established in medical practice, and facilities are available in the UK in nearly all acute hospitals. The physician wishing to become a consultant in nuclear medicine should be interested in all aspect of clinical medicine, and usually will have a special interest in physiology, alterations in function due to disease, and in basic science.

The consultant's job

Historically, nuclear medicine services in the UK have been provided by consultants in nuclear medicine, by radiologists with special interest in radionuclide imaging, and by other clinicians who wish to utilise nuclear medicine procedures for their own specialty (for instance some cardiologists, endocrinologists and oncologists). The diversity of the specialty means that the nuclear medicine consultant has to work closely with a wide variety of clinical specialists, and with others providing diagnostic services such as radiologists and pathologists. The ability to liaise closely with these different groups is one of the greatest challenges for the nuclear medicine specialist. A nuclear medicine physician may wish to specialise in particular areas, such as cardiology, thyroid work or positron emission tomography (PET scanning). The unique ability to study physiology and pathological process by non-invasive methods means that nuclear medicine procedures are used extensively for research. The central responsibility of the specialist will, however, continue to be the provision of a diagnostic and therapeutic clinical service.

Training requirements

The training requirements are contained in the curriculum for higher specialist training in nuclear medicine published by the Joint Committee of Higher Medical Training (JCHMT). Those entering higher medical training programmes should have completed a minimum of two years General Professional Training (GPT) in approved posts and obtained the

MRCP(UK) or FRCR. The duration of higher medical training in nuclear medicine is four years and will be provided in approved centres. Those entering with FRCR may be exempt for up to 2 years of this training programme.

Career prospects

Whilst nuclear medicine procedures are widely available in acute hospitals in the UK, the organisation of these services has developed in many areas in an ad hoc way. This situation is changing and it has been recognised there is a need to provide more fully trained specialists particularly for larger centres. Career prospects are excellent for those entering the profession, and the limited acute on-call commitment makes nuclear medicine an attractive specialty for those who wish to train or practise part time.

Further information

Specialist Advisory Committee for Nuclear Medicine
Royal College of Physicians
11 St Andrews Place
Regent's Park
London NW1 4LE
Tel: 020 7935 1174
Fax: 020 7486 4160
Website: www.rcplondon.ac.uk/jchmt

Occupational medicine

Occupational medicine is concerned with the effects of work on health and the effects of health on the ability to work. There is an extensive health and safety regulatory framework within the UK and the European Union, which has encouraged many employers to provide occupational health services. The majority of these operate outside the National Health Service and many senior occupational physicians may have a multi-national role.

The Faculty of Occupational Medicine is responsible for specialist training and standards of practice in occupational medicine in the UK. It has more than 1,300 Fellows, Members and Associates. The Society of Occupational Medicine provides professional representation through regional groups. It has over 1,800 members.

The occupational physician's role

The specialist's role is to advise workers, management and trade unions on all health matters with the aim of preventing work-related disease and promoting good health. This is a clinical and preventative discipline requiring a detailed knowledge of occupational diseases and expertise in health assessment, rehabilitation, toxicology, environmental assessment and control, and the application of epidemiological techniques. As industries evolve, new working environments and exposures may create new health hazards and fitness requirements. The shift from manual to knowledge based industries has given greater importance to occupational mental health with a need for good behavioural and psychological skills.

The problem of different industries – eg engineering, transport, retail, food, chemical, mining and health care – has lead to much sub-specialisation. As well as the experience described, the occupational physician also needs to acquire managerial and communication skills in order to operate effectively within a commercial environment and work with managers and employee groups. The majority of occupational physician's work is outside the NHS although the number of specialists and specialist registrar posts in the NHS is increasing.

Occupational health facilities vary, depending upon the nature of the industry, but normally include provision for the treatment of illness and injury at work, for occupational health assessment and surveillance, and often physiotherapy or rehabilitation services. The majority of occupational health physicians work either in small groups or singly, but usually with occupational health nurses. The effective provision of occupational health services depends upon teamwork with other related disciplines such as occupational nurses, safety practitioners and hygienists. Epidemiology and research are important to identify and assess work-related hazards to health.

Training requirements

Entry to the specialty is after the completion of general professional training. The gaining of MRCGP or MRCP (UK) is desirable, although not mandatory. Training can only be undertaken in posts approved by the Faculty of Occupational Medicine and all trainees must have a personal supervisor who is a member of the Faculty.

Each trainee has a personal training programme approved by the Faculty, which is designed to ensure progress towards acquiring the clinical, technical and managerial competencies required to become a specialist. This normally lasts for four years, or pro-rata where flexible training has been permitted for well-founded reasons

The Associateship of the Faculty is gained by examination, which is normally taken after two years of training, and membership is awarded after submission of a satisfactory dissertation and the completion of training. Annual appraisals of training progress are conducted by the postgraduate dean and then reported to the Faculty.

Satisfactory completion of training and award of the MFOM leads to the issue of a Certificate of Completion of Specialist Training (CCST).

Career prospects

There are over 100 specialist registrars training in occupational medicine and about 140 approved training posts, with about 75 per cent of all trainees and posts being outside the NHS in the private sector. Trained occupational physicians with wide experience are in demand and can look forward to a challenging and rewarding career.

Further information

The Faculty of Occupational Medicine
6 St Andrews Place
Regent's Park
London NW1 4LB
Tel: 020 7317 5890
Fax: 020 7317 5899
E-mail: FOM@facoccmed.ac.uk

The Society of Occupational Medicine
6 St Andrew's Place
Regent's Park
London NW1 4LB
Tel: 020 7486 2641
Fax: 020 7486 0028
E-mail: SOM@sococcmed.demon.co.uk

Palliative medicine

Palliative medicine is the medical care of patients with progressive incurable disease, particularly those in the later stages of their illness. Although the majority of patients have malignant disease, an increasing proportion have other conditions such as motor neurone disease, HIV disease or cardiac or respiratory failure. Doctors who wish to work in palliative medicine will require a sound training in general medicine and a broad understanding of the treatment of primary and secondary malignant disease including medical, surgical and radiotherapeutic approaches to treatment. They will also need to understand the importance of meeting their patients' psychological needs as well as their physical ones, and of caring for families in bereavement. Good palliative care is based on interdisciplinary teamwork. It is therefore essential both to understand and to respect the skills of non-medical colleagues. Patients may be cared for in primary care settings, acute hospitals, and nursing homes or in hospices or specialist palliative care inpatient units. An understanding of the advantages and disadvantages of care outside the acute hospital is therefore required.

The consultant's job

The consultant in palliative medicine will provide the highest possible standard of medical care for patients in all settings, with particular emphasis on the rapid and effective control of pain and other distressing symptoms. In addition to carrying responsibility for the ongoing care of patients, he or she will often act in an advisory role, sharing the care of patients both in the community and in acute hospitals. The consultant's role will include regularly reviewing the evidence for medical procedures and drug therapy, keeping abreast of research developments and leading the development of protocols for the management of pain and other symptoms. He or she will also be a member of the interdisciplinary team which assesses and seeks to deal with the emotional, social and spiritual needs of patients and families. Teaching is an integral part of the consultant's role and consultants are increasingly involved in the development and management of specialist palliative care services.

Training requirements

Applicants for training need to have completed a minimum of two years general professional training leading to MRCP(UK), FRCR (Clinical Oncology) or FRCA, or in a general practitioner vocational training scheme leading to MRCGP. Experience in palliative medicine or in oncology is an advantage. The duration of training is four years, of which at least two must be spent in specialist palliative medicine. Training is organised so that the trainee experiences the full range of services in different settings, including inpatient care, day care, hospital support, home care and bereavement services. At least one year of training may be spent in general medicine or in relevant specialties, eg oncology, infection, radiotherapy, haematology, geriatric medicine, pain manage-ment or in a training post approved for this purpose in general practice. Research experience is encouraged and up to one year can be incorp-orated into the training programme; trainees may wish to step aside from the programme for a longer period in order to complete a higher degree. By the completion of the four-year programme the trainee must have demonstrated competence across the whole curriculum of specialist palliative medicine. The training programme is not linked with training in general internal medicine.

Career prospects

Career prospects in palliative medicine are good and there is much competition for training posts. Although there has been a considerable expansion in the number of training posts in the specialty there is a continuing expansion in consultant numbers. At present, a significant number of consultant posts advertised attract no candidates. Many consultant posts are single-handed. This is increasingly recognised as undesirable, and unsustainable in the long term. The need to develop second and subsequent consultant posts in these services is likely to drive a continued expansion in consultant numbers for some years.

Further information

Specialist Advisory Committee for Palliative Medicine
Royal College of Physicians
11 St Andrews Place
Regent's Park
London NW1 4LE
Tel: 020 7935 1174
Fax: 020 7486 4160
Website: www.rcplondon.ac.uk/jchmt
Secretary: Dr J Wiles
Secretariat: Cath Janion

Pharmaceutical medicine

Pharmaceutical medicine is a medical scientific discipline concerned with the discovery, development, evaluation, registration, monitoring and medical aspects of marketing of medicines for the benefit of patients and the public health.

Jobs in pharmaceutical medicine

Careers in pharmaceutical medicine encompass three main groups of physicians: those working in the pharmaceutical industry, those with appointments within regulatory bodies such as the Medicines Control Agency (MCA) and those working in independent research organisations dedicated to the development of new medicines. As very few of the jobs in the discipline conform to a conventional medical structure there is no clear-cut point where a fully trained pharmaceutical physician becomes a consultant. Similarly there is a wide range of jobs with different levels of responsibilities ranging from the director of the MCA and industry divisional heads with hundreds or even thousands of staff through to medical directors in specialist areas with one or two assistants. The jobs with greater responsibilities require not only training in basic pharmaceutical medicine but also many years of experience and dedication. Such pharmaceutical physicians also need to acquire highly developed skills in financial and other aspects of management.

There are several subdisciplines in pharmaceutical medicine which include:

▶ research and development – working on drugs before they are on the market
▶ medical services – working on drugs which are on the market
▶ drug safety surveillance – dealing with adverse events of drugs both in research and on the market
▶ regulatory affairs – working on submissions either for the regulatory agencies or in the agencies themselves.

One pharmaceutical physician may be responsible, with his or her team, for all the clinical development for one or more compounds. The development programme must effectively evaluate the risk/benefit which can be a major challenge in a discipline which is by definition always working on the frontiers of science. It is essential that good communication be maintained across the world so that effective and efficient drug development can be conducted and adverse event surveillance can be maintained within companies and regulatory authorities.

Training requirements

Prospective entrants to HMT in pharmaceutical medicine will have completed a minimum of two years GPT in approved Senior House Officer (SHO) posts following full registration. It is highly recommended, but not obligatory, for a doctor embarking on a career in pharmaceutical medicine to be in possession of a scientific qualification (eg BSc) and/or a post-graduate medical or scientific diploma or degree (eg MSc, PhD, MD, MRCP(UK), MRCPath).

HMT will provide the trainee with the experience of all the main aspects of pharmaceutical medicine. The individualised (*ad personam*) training programme to which the trainee signs up will be approved by the Faculty and by the Specialist Advisory Committee on Pharmaceutical Medicine (SAC-PM).

This consists of a two-year programme of basic training, covering the core curriculum of the syllabus in pharmaceutical medicine and leading to the Diploma in Pharmaceutical Medicine of the Faculty of Pharmaceutical Medicine. The Diploma is part of the regulations for Associateship of the Faculty (AFPM).

A two-year modular programme of advanced training in six fields of practice in pharmaceutical medicine follows or accompanies basic training. The modular training is conducted either through work-place experience or is course-based. A senior specialty adviser, appointed jointly by the postgraduate dean, the Faculty and the SAC-PM, and a nominated educational supervisor at the place of work, who is normally the trainee's immediate manager, form the core training team, who, together with the trainee, construct and oversee the training programme.

Throughout HMT, trainees should acquire and maintain a thorough knowledge of the principles and practices of the management of diseases in the therapeutic areas in which they are working. They should acquire investigational skills in those areas of applied clinical research covered by the training programme. They should also acquire a thorough understanding of the administration and management of those organisations in which they work or with which they are affiliated within pharmaceutical medicine.

Completion of specialist training follows the completion of the training programme of HMT, which permits candidates to apply for Membership of the Faculty (MFPM), which is the exit criterion of specialist training. Approval is awaited from the Department of Health for a CCST in pharmaceutical medicine.

Career prospects

Many pharmaceutical physicians trained in the UK now live in North America or in continental European countries (currently estimated at over 20 per cent) illustrating the truly international nature of the discipline. There are many exciting career opportunities within the subject; most carry a great deal of sometimes exhilarating responsibility which may not be readily apparent. Most are part of large organisations (pharmaceutical companies or government departments) and are just as subject to organisational policies and structural hierarchies as the NHS or academia.

Further information

Please contact in the first instance:
Faculty of Pharmaceutical Medicine
1 St Andrews Place
Regent's Park
London NW1 4LB
Tel: 020 7224 0343
Fax: 020 7224 5381

Public health medicine

Public health physicians have two main roles. They assess the health and well-being of communities and they contribute to the planning, delivery and evaluation of health services and other activities which aim to protect, promote and improve health.

The consultant's job

Public health is a multi-disciplinary activity. Public health physicians share generic skills with specialists from other disciplines, such as economics, statistics and social sciences. Their medical training and experience in hospitals and community services help them to work closely with clinical colleagues to develop, improve and monitor services to patients. In addition, public health physicians often need to discuss individual patient care arrangements with clinicians, so it is essential that they maintain close contact and up-to-date knowledge on clinical issues.

The health of the population is affected by many factors which are the responsibility of other agencies – environmental matters, housing, education and employment. Public health physicians therefore have to be able to work in a wide arena, spanning central and local governments, universities, industry, public and private health care. They advise on the public health impact of proposals and policies and seek to influence decision-makers in favour of healthy choices.

In the UK every health authority or health board has a public health physician as director of public health or chief administrative medical officer, heading a multi-professional team which includes physicians at consultant level and in training grades. A major focus for the work of these public health teams is the development and implementation of health improvement programmes for their local community.

Training requirements

The award of the Certificate of Completion of Specialist Training in public health medicine requires the satisfactory completion of four years training in approved SpR posts, after at least three years of general professional training. An increasing number of SHO posts are now available for those wishing to have some experience of public health medicine or to prepare to enter formal training. An extensive series of competencies must be acquired during the SpR period, together with experience in the practice of public health medicine in a variety of settings. Overseas experience (for example in Europe or in developing countries) and experience outside the NHS are also encouraged. Special focuses are possible in training, for example communicable diseases or academic epidemiology, although there are no formal sub-specialties within the CCST in public health medicine. Individuals who enter public health medicine with extensive relevant clinical or research experience may be able to shorten the length of their training programme and may be entitled to salary protection.

During training SpRs will be required to pass the membership examination of the Faculty of Public Health Medicine. The Diploma and Part 1 Membership examination (with the award of Diplomate Membership – DFPHM) will be taken within the first year or two of training, or even before entry. Many specialist registrars have the opportunity to attend formal academic courses (full-time or part-time, often leading to the award of a Master's degree) to help prepare for the Part 1 examination. The Part 2 Membership examination, taken near the end of training, involves demonstration of a set of competencies by means of written reports of work, and oral examinations on the practice of public health medicine.

Career prospects

The numbers of national training numbers in public health medicine in the UK have continued to increase because there are growing opportunities and needs for consultants in a wide variety of posts – in late 1997 there were about 100 vacant NHS consultant posts in public health medicine in the UK. Increasing opportunities for public health practice within primary care also means that there are real possibilities for individuals to combine the practice of public health medicine with clinical general practice. Dual accreditation with other clinical specialties is also under consideration.

Further information

Full details of education and training in public health medicine, and contacts for enquiries, are available on the website of the Faculty of Public Health Medicine:

Website: http://fester.his.path.cam.ac.uk/phealth/fphm.htm

Rehabilitation medicine

Rehabilitation medicine is the specialty which aims to assist disabled people in achieving and maintaining optimal physical, mental and social functioning. This is a very broad and challenging agenda and involves not only conventional medical skills but using all means to reduce the impact of disabling conditions; this may include prescribing assistive devices, changing environments and influencing social attitudes.

The consultant's job

One of the hallmarks of rehabilitation medicine is inter-disciplinary teamwork. The team(s) may involve colleagues from education, employment, engineering, social services and the voluntary sector, as well as nurses, therapists and psychologists. The consultant must therefore be a good team player, capable of communicating clearly, of motivating as well as leading, and be able to negotiate and fight for resources and facilities. The medical responsibilities will include ensuring the diagnosis is properly explained, treating symptoms, and preventing complications, as well as empowering the disabled individual as far as possible.

The exact duties of the post vary enormously. Although the specialty evolved to meet the needs of the '16–65 age group', some areas such as amputee rehabilitation, orthotics and wheelchairs, cover all age groups. The interfaces with paediatric rehabilitation, particularly assisting disabled school leavers, is immensely rewarding. In the adult age group, returning a person to the community after traumatic brain injury, reducing spasticity in a person with multiple sclerosis, or assessing for environmental control units, all present their own challenges. Transitional arrangements with elderly care services will need to remain flexible as demographic changes dictate patterns of care.

Historically rehabilitation medicine posts have been in acute settings but increasingly future posts will span acute and community trusts as 'seamless provision of care' becomes established. In the past, some dual appointments were made with such specialties as neurology and rheumatology, but rehabilitation tended to get sidelined by the pressures of more 'acute' work. It is now the norm for consultants to practice exclusively in rehabilitation medicine.

Training requirements

Entry into higher medical training in rehabilitation medicine starts after completion of general professional training and gaining an appropriate postgraduate degree. Experience in neurology, rheumatology and geriatric medicine or rehabilitation medicine are all desirable, but not essential. The minimum duration of training in rehabilitation medicine is four years. The training includes seven obligatory areas, such as neurological rehabilitation, spinal injuries and areas of assistive technology, as well as psychological, organisation and management issues. Otherwise there is a wide range of flexibility with many options available. Exposure to the breadth of the specialty is encouraged and duplication should be avoided. Up to a year may be spent in research. For fuller details, see the JCHMT Handbook for Rehabilitation Medicine.

Career prospects

Career prospects in rehabilitation medicine are excellent. This is a relatively new specialty (established in 1989) and is expanding rapidly. Presently it is proving difficult to fill all the consultant posts being advertised because of the previous dearth of training grades. The number of SpR posts has been increased from 45 in 1998 to 65 in 1999 and needs further expansion to meet the aim of one consultant per 250,000 of the population.

The breadth of the specialty means there are many diverse opportunities and the challenges of working with complex teams can be very rewarding. There is ample scope for research, both in evaluating existing techniques and developing new measurement tools and assistive devices. The academic base of the specialty is expanding and there are now nine academic chairs. There are several specialist societies for presentation of research and to fulfil CME requirements.

As 'on call' in the specialty need not be particularly onerous, Rehabilitation Medicine lends itself well to flexible working arrangements, which would suit those unable to take on full-time commitments.

Further information

British Society of Rehabilitation Medicine (BSRM)
c/o Royal College of Physicians
11 St Andrews Place
Regent's Park
London NW1 4LE
Tel/Fax: 01992 638865   *continued over*

E-mail: bsrm@b.t.connect.com
Website: bsrm.co.uk (imminent)

The Society for Research in Rehabilitation (SRR)
Stroke Medicine
Clinical Services Building
City Hospital
Hucknall Road
Nottingham NG5 1PB
Tel: 0115 9691169
Fax: 0115 8404790
E-mail: ann.hughes@nottingham.ac.uk
          john.gladman@nottingham.ac.uk
Website: (currently in) http://www.nottingham.ac.uk

Amputee Medical Rehabilitation Society (AMRS)
Address as for BSRM

International Society for Prosthetics and Orthotics (ISPO)
UK National Member Society
PO Box 26528
London SE3 7NF

Posture and Mobility Group
c/o Eur. Ing. Roy Nelham (Chairman)
Director of Rehabilitation Engineering and Clinical Science
Chailey Heritage
Beggars Wood Road
North Chailey
Lewes
East Sussex BN8 4JN
Tel: 01825 722112
Fax: 01825 724 261
E-mail: roynelham@compuserve.com

Specialist Advisory Committee for Rehabilitation Medicine
Royal College of Physicians
11 St Andrews Place
Regent's Park
London NW1 4LE
Tel: 020 7935 1174
Fax: 020 7486 4160
Website: www.rcplondon.ac.uk/jchmt
Secretary: Dr C Collin

Renal medicine

The relatively low incidence of renal disease within the population means that extensive clinical experience in this specialty is denied to physicians in other disciplines. However renal disorders often complicate multisystem diseases such as diabetes so that all physicians should have knowledge of nephrology and conversely renal physicians need an extensive experience in general medicine. The management and investigation of hypertension and of metabolic disorders often falls to the nephrologist, broadening the scope of the specialty. With the increased need for regular dialysis many district general hospitals now provide full renal services including dialysis, although renal transplantation is usually confined to regional teaching hospitals. Satellite dialysis units managed from the main renal units are being established often within smaller hospitals to provide treatment close to the patient's home. The nature of the specialty ensures a broad base for clinical and laboratory research.

The consultant's job

The consultant works as one of a team of consultants, single-handed nephrologists are becoming a thing of the past. Much of the consultant's work is outpatient based and may involve satellite clinics at other hospitals. Supervision of the day to day running of a large renal unit in terms of acute admissions, hospital referrals and the routine investigation of patients is often on a rotational basis with consultant colleagues. This allows 'reservoirs' of time to pursue specialist clinical interests or research. There is close integration with other disciplines, including diagnostic radiology, nuclear medicine, immunology, pathology and urology. The renal unit relies on a cohesive structure with highly trained nursing and technical support staff and with the increasingly 'industrialised' haemodialysis unit, the development of administrative skills on the part of the clinician has become very important. In large units there is a trend towards renal physicians not undertaking acute general medicine because of the increasing nephrology workload. In smaller units participation in general medicine is the norm. Junior staff in small units are often less experienced in nephrology and the practical skills of the consultant are more frequently called upon.

Training requirements

Aspiring nephrologists may train only in nephrology or jointly in nephrology and general internal medicine (GIM). The training requirements for pure nephrology registration are for a period of 3 years of full time clinical training in nephrology plus a fourth year which may be in research, GIM, a related specialty or a further year of nephrology. For joint specialisation in GIM and nephrology, three years of clinical nephrology and two years of clinical GIM training are required. Although a period of supervised research is not obligatory for specialist registration, it is considered highly desirable. Since most trainees opt for joint training in GIM and nephrology, and most will undertake full time research at some point in their training, it seems likely that the time spent in the SpR grade will often be six or seven years.

Career prospects

Currently there are 230 consultant posts in renal medicine in the United Kingdom. The consultant expansion rate was 16 per cent per annum from 1992–1996, and although it fell to 3.4 per cent for the year 1997–98, it is planned to be approximately 11 per cent per annum over the next 5 years. This expansion is required to meet the needs of an increasing dialysis population and to accommodate the change to a consultant based service together with increased teaching of trainees. If this planned consultant expansion is achieved, then the output of trained nephrologists will match the posts available over the 5 year period. This expansion in consultant posts is essential to bring us into line with the provision in other European countries.

Further Information

The Renal Association
Honorary Secretary: Dr THJ Goodship
                    Department of Medicine
                    University of Newcastle
                    (until September 2000)
Website: http://www.renal.org

Specialist Advisory Committee for Renal Medicine
Royal College of Physicians
11 St Andrews Place
Regent's Park
London NW1 4LE
Tel: 020 7935 1174
Fax: 020 7486 4160
Website: www.rcplondon.ac.uk/jchmt
Secretary: Dr D Carmichael
Secretariat: Kate Forrester

Respiratory medicine

Respiratory medicine comprises approximately 25 per cent of all general medicine, ie patients admitted through emergency departments on acute unselected medical take. It is therefore an interesting mixture of acute general medicine and investigative practice. The main diseases for the respiratory physician include chronic airflow obstruction, asthma, lung cancer, tuberculosis and the host infiltrative lung diseases.

The consultant's job

Most respiratory physicians partake in unselected medical take or are at least involved in the immediate care of acute respiratory problems admitted through casualty. There is always an active consultative service on respiratory problems within a large hospital. The respiratory physician should be an expert fibre-optic bronchoscopist, a good interpreter of chest X-rays, CT and MRI scans. Most respiratory physicians participate in the running of lung function testing laboratories. Most institutions will also have a separate clinic for TB that is run by the respiratory physician. Rarer diseases, such as occupational lung disease, cystic fibrosis, non-invasive domiciliary ventilation and the management of immuno-compromised patients are carried out in regional or separate units.

Respiratory physicians are responsible for two to five outpatient clinics per week, including general medicine, new thoracic patients, follow up clinics, asthma clinics, lung cancer clinics and tuberculosis clinics. Sleep disordered breathing is a rapidly evolving field that lies appropriately within the province of the respiratory physician. There should be adequate local facilities, or at least in a nearby centre, for the investigation and treatment of Obstructive Sleep Apnoea (OSA).

Training requirements

The Calman training programme has a clear-cut four year training programme in respiratory and general internal medicine. Approximately two years are formally designated to each. Most posts, however, contain a combination of general medicine as well as thoracic medicine, both counting towards training. A fifth research year is available, but it is encouraged for most serious trainees to do a three year programme as an MD or PhD.

Each region has its established rotations in respiratory disease with two years more heavily involved in acute internal medicine and unselected take, and the other two years, in a centre where respiratory medicine predominates over general. Training is now carefully supervised, with a training day once a month as well as other formal sessions. Training centres provide facilities for bronchoscopy, tuberculosis, sleep disordered breathing, a multi-disciplinary lung cancer clinic, lung function testing and its interpretation, asthma clinics, sarcoidosis and interstitial lung disease clinics. Regional centres provide expertise in laser bronchoscopy, rigid bronchoscopy, stenting and brachytherapy. Cystic fibrosis, non-invasive ventilation and intensive care, can also be provided in some centres. Most centres will have weekly meetings to discuss interesting radiology, histopathology meetings, physiological teaching meetings as well as research in progress sessions. The teaching of junior medical staff and of undergraduates is implicit in most training programmes as part of the day-to-day life of that centre. Research for a higher degree, preferably a PhD, is actively encouraged and these should be pursued by the candidate in a centre where there is an active programme and most importantly, very careful and regular supervision.

Career prospects

Currently there are more than adequate numbers of NTN's in Respiratory medicine but there is likely to be a surfeit of consultant posts coming available between the years 2002 and 2006. The number of respiratory physicians in the UK is 1 per 115,000 population and the European recommendation is 1 for 60,000 people. The current aim is to reduce the number to 1 in 80,000 and it is hoped therefore that respiratory medicine consultant posts will expand at about 6 per cent per annum.

Further information

British Thoracic Society
6th Floor
North Wing
New Garden House
78 Hatton Garden
London EC1N 8LD
Tel: 020 7831 8778
Fax: 020 7831 8766
Website: www.brit-thoracic.org.uk

Specialist Advisory Committee for Respiratory Medicine
Royal College of Physicians
11 St Andrews Place
Regent's Park
London NW1 4LE
Tel: 020 7935 1174
Fax: 020 7486 4160
Website: www.rcplondon.ac.uk/jchmt
Secretary: Professor M Hodson
Secretariat: Kate Hope

Rheumatology

There are over 200 different rheumatic diseases recognised in the United Kingdom, affecting people of any age and covering congenital, inflammatory, metabolic and degenerative processes. The conditions are very common, accounting for up to a quarter of attendances at general practitioner surgeries, although clearly only a proportion need a specialist opinion. Many rheumatic diseases affect other systems than the musculoskeletal and demand a wide experience of general medicine. The scope of rheumatic diseases is such that, whilst many doctors specialise in rheumatology alone, others choose to be involved in related fields such as immunology, genetics or general (internal) medicine.

The consultant's job

About three-quarters of established consultant posts are in rheumatology alone. However over recent years trusts and other employers have sought to appoint a general physician with special expertise in rheumatology with the aim that the consultant will take his share of the acute general admissions as well as spending most of his working week doing rheumatology.

All rheumatologists can expect to have access to inpatient beds for the care of those with the most active and sometimes life threatening disease processes. Some can expect to be part of clearly defined departments often with a number of protected beds and sometimes a close association with orthopaedic surgeons who have much to contribute to the long-term care and management of patients with chronic arthritis. In such settings, it is often easier to organise the necessary team work with other health professionals such as specialist nurses, physiotherapists, and occupational therapists who can do so much to ensure the delivery of optimum patient care to often disadvantaged patients.

Much of the work of a rheumatology department is done in the outpatient clinic where the support may come not only from the health professional team but also staff grade doctors rather than junior staff in training. Most outpatient clinics are hospital based, but over recent years there has been increased demand to undertake outreach clinics in both community hospitals and general practitioners surgeries. Life threatening crises and long-term care of patients with rheumatic disease require skilled management and close co-operation with colleagues in other disciplines and professions. Thus it is important to have had a broad-based training programme and to understand the skills that others can bring to the care of your patient.

Training requirements

Specialist registrar rotations are now widely established in the United Kingdom with each offering an extensive range of clinical and research experience. Most training rotations can lead to dual accreditation in rheumatology and general (internal) medicine. If the trainee plans to undertake appropriate research and study towards a higher degree then it is necessary to take time out from that training programme. This should be straightforward, but it is important to discuss these plans with the educational advisory team at an early stage. Research may be clinical or laboratory based, covering such diverse fields as biochemistry, biomechanics, epidemiology, genetics, immunology, molecular biology and pharmacology. Academic units and other large rheumatology centres have specialist interests and will be able to advise on funding and supervision of work in their field.

The British Society for Rheumatology (BSR) organises scientific meetings and basic and advanced educational courses. It continues to liaise closely with other bodies on manpower levels and training requirements. Trainee rheumatologists meet regularly and are represented on the BSR Council and its sub committees. There are also important links with training in Europe.

Career prospects

The prospects in rheumatology have improved greatly over recent years reflecting the value that general practitioners, with their ability to influence health-purchasing decisions, have placed on rheumatology services. Based upon a suggested need for one rheumatologist per 85,000 of population, there is scope for further expansion and certainly there are some areas of the country with little or no rheumatology service. All doctors in the future can expect to be involved in management and administration and to be familiar with the issues involved in purchasing and providing medical services. Accordingly, alongside any administrative ability, teaching skills and a willingness to participate in postgraduate training at all levels are also much valued.

Further Information

The British Society for Rheumatology,
41 Eagle Street,
London WC1R 4AR.

Specialist Advisory Committee for Rheumatology
Royal College of Physicians
11 St Andrews Place
Regent's Park
London NW1 4LE
Tel: 020 7935 1174
Fax: 020 7486 4160
Website: www.rcplondon.ac.uk/jchmt
Secretary: Dr E Tunn
Secretariat: Kate Hope